Nature's *Weather* Forecasters

Nature's Weather Forecasters

HELEN R. SATTLER

THOMAS NELSON INC., PUBLISHERS
Nashville   New York

First edition

Library of Congress Cataloging in Publication Data

Sattler, Helen Roney.
    Nature's weather forecasters.

    Includes index.
    SUMMARY: Describes nature's weather indicators which, in many cases, are more accurate than the forecasts of the United States Weather Bureau.
    1. Weather forecasting—Juvenile literature.
2. Nature—Juvenile literature. [1. Weather forecasting 2. Nature] I. Title.
QC995.43.S27   551.6′3   78-1694
ISBN 0-8407-6594-0

to
my husband Bob
who has brought more sunshine
than rain into my life

Contents

Nature's Weather Forecasters

One

Weather Wisdom

"Shep tried to warn us, but we wouldn't listen," sobbed a fourteen-year-old girl from her hospital bed after a tornado struck her home.

Shep never came into the house, but that afternoon he had nearly knocked the door down trying to get in. He had run from one family member to another, jumping up on them, whining and crying.

"As if he were trying to tell us something," the girl said later.

The family was puzzled by his behavior. The dog had never acted that way before.

"The radio report forecast severe thunderstorms, but hadn't mentioned a twister," her father explained. "Shep knows we always go to the cellar when there is a tornado warning. Somehow he knew one was coming and tried to get us there."

Animals, especially dogs, behave strangely just before a storm.

This family learned something their ancestors had known for hundreds of years. Before the United States Weather Bureau began issuing alerts in 1948, people in the plains area, where tornadoes are most frequent, depended upon nature to warn them of approaching tornadoes. Dark, ominous clouds that bubbled and boiled in greenish skies, the peculiar behavior of animals, especially dogs, or a rumbling roar like that of a heavily loaded freight train—such signs would send them scurrying to their storm cellars.

Severe storms and tornadoes often form so rapidly that the Weather Bureau doesn't have time to warn all the people in a storm path to take cover. But, like a rattlesnake, nature does not strike without some advance warning. No matter where you are, you can get a surprisingly accurate forecast of the weather for the next few hours just by being observant. In many cases nature's weather predictors are more accurate than the United States Weather Bureau. The reason for this accuracy may be that animals are constantly assessing the conditions *in their own particular territory*, whereas the Bureau makes predictions for 12-to-36-hour periods, covering areas of 150 to 200 square miles. Birds, mammals, and insects seem to sense that they could lose their lives if they are wrong.

Violent storms have always been a threat to people, as well, and they must have been much more terrifying to our ancestors than they are to us. In the past, people had no weather bureau to warn them when to take cover, and they had little protection if they were caught in a severe storm. Therefore, they looked for ways to protect themselves against the weather.

A long time ago, when people lived mostly out-of-doors, they were very close to nature. They soon noticed that plants, mammals, insects, and birds sensed the coming of a storm sooner than people do. All living things have a natural instinct to save their own lives, and so they look for shelter just before a storm. Therefore, when ancient peoples saw animals seeking shelter, they did, too.

For centuries farmers and sailors studied and observed nature and weather. They observed that plants and animals behave in odd and unusual ways just before a storm. By watching them, people learned to predict storms nearly as accurately as modern weathermen can.

This was an important discovery, because people then were even more at the mercy of the weather than we are today. Sailors and fishermen depended upon nature's weather forecasters to tell them when it was safe to go to sea, since their small boats could not ride out a severe storm. When sailing vessels were invented, weather knowledge became even more important. Throughout history admirals of ships used weather wisdom to help win battles at sea.

The British seamen's superior ability to read the weather signs gave them an advantage over the formidable Spanish Armada and contributed to their victory. Had the Spanish admirals been as familiar with the habits of the prevailing westerlies as they were with the trade-winds region, they would not have sailed into the treacherous English Channel that stormy July in 1588.

In the past, farmers depended upon nature to warn them when to bring in their herds or reap their crops. A warning of a storm often meant the difference between starvation and enough food to last their families through the winter. Hunting and gathering people laid in larger stocks if animals and plants told them the winter would be long and severe.

Of course, plants and animals do not actually forecast weather, but they are good weather indicators. Although the farmers and sailors of former times didn't know it, their weather wisdom was just as correct as that of modern meteorologists (scientists who study weather), who collect weather information with complicated scientific instruments. The elements that make up weather—barometric pressure, moisture, temperature, and wind—have an effect upon plants and animals. Living things show these effects in special ways, and the way they act gives clues to weather changes. The people of long ago called these clues "weather signs."

Weather signs were a little different from one country to another, but people all over the world had suitable ones for their own area. The ancient Babylonians were the first people we know about who studied nature to forecast weather. They collected thousands of omens and wrote them down on clay tablets. Some of these tablets still exist. The ancient Egyptians also wrote about weather signs. Aristotle, a philosopher of ancient Greece, wrote a book about weather lore around the year 330 B.C. One of his pupils, Theophrastus, spent most of his life recording weather signs. Many of the signs that he recorded have been handed down to us nearly unchanged.

Even before the pyramids were built in Egypt, weather signs were passed down from one generation to another. Joseph must have taught them to Jesus, because Jesus quotes one in the New Testament: "When it is evening, you say, 'It will be fair weather; for the sky is red.' And in the morning, 'It will be stormy today, for the sky is red and threatening' " (Matthew 16:2–3).

When early settlers came to this country they were amazed by the ability of the American Indians to pre-

dict disastrous storms. When one of the worst hur-
ricanes in history hit Florida, the Seminole Indians,
who lived there, knew four days in advance that it was
going to strike. They moved to a safe place, and so
avoided a catastrophe. It has been said that successful
rain dancers read the weather signs before they began
their dances so they could be sure of success.

A hundred years ago, rural and coastal children in
America grew up knowing weather signs. Fathers and
mothers taught this valuable information to their children. Today very few people in America know the
weather signs. Most people live in cities, and they have
forgotten weather signs. Almost everyone, even in
rural areas, depends upon meteorological reports in the
daily newspaper, on television, or on radio to keep
himself informed about weather conditions.

But weather wisdom is still useful. Anyone who
flies a small airplane, goes camping, climbs mountains,
takes bike hikes, backpacks in the woods, sails a boat,
or goes anywhere that takes him out of touch with
television or radio needs to have at least a little weather
sense. Weather is constantly changing. It is possible for
a storm to develop very rapidly. By learning to read
weather signs you can get a few hours' advance warning
if a storm is headed your way. It might save your life.

Weather knowledge might also save a crop. A man
who had lived in the city all his life and then decided to
move to the country learned that the hard way. He
bought a farm and planted his crops. But time and time
again his hay was rained on after it was cut, then rotted
in the field. His corn either froze in the spring or didn't
ripen before frost.

"Jake," he asked his neighbor, "how come I'm having such bad luck?"

"Sam," replied Jake, "you aren't having bad luck. You just don't have any weather sense."

"What do you mean?"

"Well, you cut your hay when the robin is in the bush and plant your corn before the oaks leaf. Nobody can make a crop if he doesn't read the signs. Everyone knows a robin in the bush means it's going to rain, and that you shouldn't plant corn until the oak leaves are as big as a mouse's ear."

The next year, Sam followed his neighbors advice, and his corn and hay did well.

Weather signs can also prevent you from coming home shivering or soaked to the skin.

Weather changes do not happen without warnings well in advance. These warnings are the weather signs that farmers, shepherds, sailors, and all people close to nature, such as Indians, knew in the past. Anyone can learn them. All around you there are clues to weather changes. Train your eyes to see them. Learn some basic weather facts, and you will see some signs each time you walk outdoors. Study birds, mammals, and insects under normal conditions. Then you will be aware of the changes in their behavior that can warn you of approaching bad weather.

No matter where you live, you will find many kinds of creatures. Even in a big city there are ants, fleas, roaches, flies, crickets, spiders, sparrows, starlings, and pigeons. There are cats, dogs, squirrels, mice, and rats. If you look closely, you can find rabbits, chipmunks, and a variety of birds in a park or open field.

Each of these creatures will be busily trying to stay alive in its own environment. Life is full of dangers. All around are other creatures waiting for a chance to have it for dinner. The animals are safe from their enemies as long as they stay hidden in the thick ground cover of grass and dead leaves. However, a hard rain is another danger they face. No ground creature is safe in a heavy downpour. Small animals and insects must leave their hiding places and flee to higher ground.

Perhaps you have driven along a country road just before a hard rain and have seen many turtles crossing the road. Or you may have seen a dead snake, rabbit, skunk, opossum, or other small animal on the road just after a hard rain. What happened to it?

Small animals sense the coming of a heavy rain. A drop in air pressure probably alerts them to an approaching storm. In fleeing to higher ground to escape being drowned, they are often struck down by a car.

Turtles can often be seen crossing roads while they are moving to higher ground to avoid heavy rainfall.

Hawks can catch many small animals when they move to higher ground to escape being drowned in a heavy rain.

At another time you may have noticed a great number of hawks in one place, sitting on the fences or telephone wires along the road, or cruising low over a field, often dropping to the ground after prey. Hawks, who feed upon small animals, do not normally congregate in flocks. But when they sense that there will be a heavy rain, they wait in large numbers to take advantage of their prey's panic in order to have a good dinner. Hawks seem to know that the small animals will be fleeing to higher ground.

These are two weather signs that can forewarn you of a heavy downpour. Both are related to a sudden drop in air pressure. Meteorologists know that a sudden drop in air pressure, along with high humidity, is a sign of an approaching storm.

Two

Weather Signs and Air-Pressure Drops

Air-pressure drops affect all things, even people, as Joe Dobbs will testify. By the time Joe reached school one morning, he decided he should have stayed in bed. It was going to be "one of those days."

He broke his shoestring while dressing, knocked over a glass of milk at breakfast, was snarled at by a dog, tripped and fell flat on his face going into the school building, and on top of all that, he had forgotten his homework, which he had spent two hours preparing the night before.

Joe wasn't the only one having problems that morning.

"Another family dispute! That's three within the last hour," exclaimed the police sergeant.

"And we've had five accidents," replied another

officer. "What's got into everyone this morning?"

"Must be something in the air."

Chances are the desk sergeant wasn't far from wrong. The rash of accidents and bad luck could have been caused by a drop in atmospheric pressure. Researchers have found that there is a definite relationship between low atmospheric pressure and accidents, irritability, and forgetfulness.

The atmospheric pressure is the weight of the air pressing down upon us. Today meteorologists use a special instrument called a barometer to measure the air pressure. They keep a continuous record of its changes so that they will know when it drops and continues to drop. We have learned that the air pressure drops just before a storm and continues to drop until the storm passes.

Until the seventeenth century, people believed

Barometer

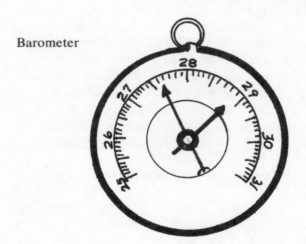

that air was weightless because Aristotle had said it was, but around 1590 Galileo, an Italian astronomer and physicist, first discovered that air had weight. One of his students, Torricelli, proved that Galileo was right and invented the barometer in 1643.

Once the barometer had been invented and people recognized a relationship between pressure drops and storms, the instrument became very popular throughout Europe. The fact that a falling barometer by itself cannot accurately predict weather didn't bother them at all. There was a barometer of some sort on every ship and in almost every home. This little rhyme helped them remember what the barometric readings meant:

> When the glass falls low,
> Prepare for a blow;
> When it rises high,
> Let all your kites fly.

Most of the time you are not aware of air pressure or its changes. Air pressure at ground level usually changes very slowly. There are times, however, when you do notice it. If you have driven up into the mountains, you know the unpleasant, stopped-up feeling in your ears as you climb higher. Air pressure decreases with an increase in altitude. As you go from the valley to the top of the mountain, the dropping air pressure causes that feeling in your ears. Going to the top of a very high building in an express elevator will sometimes make your ears pop, too. You can get the same feeling on takeoff when flying in an airplane. If you fly in an unpressurized cabin, your ears might actually hurt when the plane reaches a high altitude. Any sudden change in air pressure can cause an unpleasant feeling, ringing, or pain in your ears.

Do you ever get up feeling grumpy and all out of sorts without knowing why? Perhaps your mother or grandmother said that you got up on the wrong side of the bed. Or maybe you have noticed that on some days everyone seems grumpy. Grumpiness can be caused by a drop in air pressure and very high humidity. A sudden or greater than usual drop in air pressure can also affect your nerves. It can cause old wounds to ache, and makes corns, bunions, and arthritic joints hurt. So don't laugh when you hear an older person say, "It is going to rain. My feet hurt." He just might be right.

Hippocrates, the Greek physician who is called the Father of Medicine, taught more than two thousand years ago that there was a relationship between weather and disease. Modern medical researchers believe the reason why falling air pressure causes pain is that it makes tissues swell. This slows down blood flow and increases pressure on the brain, which triggers irritability, forgetfulness, accidents, and even violence in some people.

Although people didn't know why it happened, they knew that:

A coming storm your shooting corns presage,
And aches will throb, your hollow tooth will rage.

Theophrastus, the ancient Greek philosopher and naturalist, said, "If feet swell, the change will be to the south," because in Greece south winds often bring rain and storms.

Air-pressure drops affect other animals the same way they affect people, but most animals, being smaller, notice the effect more and sooner. If you know what to look for, you can tell when the pressure is dropping.

Just before a storm, most animals seem to be uncomfortable and act restless. They may be nervous, irritable, or even vicious. If you have a cat or dog, you may have noticed that it sometimes behaves strangely long before you can hear the distant thunder. One girl reported, "My Doberman digs a hole deep enough to bury herself. After the rain she has her own private swimming pool."

A boy said, "My spaniel crawls under a lamp table and frantically tries to dig a hole through the floor."

Some dogs will whine and crawl under the bed or in general act the same way they do after the storm has already arrived. Other dogs might act nervous or irritable and snap or snarl. An old cat acting as frisky as a kitten is said to be a sure forewarning of a storm.

The tree frog is a favorite weather forecaster in almost every country. For centuries people have believed that frogs croak longer and louder before a rain. Some say, "When the frog croaks in the meadow, it will rain in three hours." Others say, "The louder the frog, the more the rain," or:

> Frogs croak before a rain,
> But in sun stay quiet again.

Central Europeans were so sure of this that they invented a "frog barometer." A tree frog and a tiny ladder are placed in a glass jar that is half-filled with

Frog barometer

water. If the frog stays in the water and croaks, the weather will be bad. If the frog climbs up the ladder, the weather will clear. And if he stays on the top rung, the weather will stay fair. This barometer is still used in some countries.

In 1851 a British scientist named Merryweather invented a leech barometer, which he claimed was totally reliable. His storm-warning system was a jar containing twelve leeches and a bell. When bad weather approached, the leeches became active and made the bell ring. Simple leech barometers, made by placing one or more leeches in a bottle with a little water, were used in Spain for hundreds of years. If good weather was coming, the leech would remain curled up at the bottom of the bottle. If the leech crawled to the top of the bottle and stayed there, it would rain within 12 to 24 hours. If windy weather was due, the leech would move rapidly through the water and continue to do so until the wind came.

American farmers seldom owned a barometer of any kind. They preferred to use nature's weather forecasters. Many watched the chickweed, which they called the poor man's barometer, because its leaves close when the air pressure drops. Others watched their farm animals.

A Texas farmer received a good deal of publicity a few years ago when he challenged the local meteorologist to a contest to see which one of them could forecast the weather better. The farmer was right seven out of eight days, the meteorologist was correct on only four days.

Giving the credit for his accuracy to a cow and a hog, the farmer said, "It has to do with how the cow's tail acts in the morning and how deep the hog burrows into the mud."

Most farmers will tell you that when the air pressure drops suddenly, pigs squeal more than usual and sometimes frantically try to build a shelter with sticks and straw. An Oklahoma farm boy says his grandpa claims he can always tell when it will snow because his pigs begin rooting, picking up straw, and making a nest.

The country wit uses this idea to have a little fun with his neighbors. "Oh, I see it's going to snow; you have a stick in your mouth," he says every time he sees anyone with a cigar in his mouth.

This is the way some people put it:

> When pigs carry sticks,
> The clouds will play tricks;
> When they lie in the mud,
> No fears of a flood.

Pigs like to wallow in the mud to cool off in hot weather.

If a pig digs a hole in the ground, it's going to be hot. When he chews straw, it's going to rain.

And an Iowa farmer says he knows it will rain when his pigs scratch their backs on a post.

Some animals seem to make a bigger fuss than others when the air pressure drops. Ducks quack loudly, guinea hens squawk, and geese are inclined to honk more. Donkeys bray, cows bellow, and roosters crow later in the day. Old farmers say:

When the donkey blows his horn,
'Tis time to house your corn.

Don't plan a picnic if cows or chickens huddle together in clusters like football players around a quarterback, unless you like to eat in the rain. The Apache Indians say:

When cows and sheep huddle by tree and bush,
Bad weather is coming with wind and slush.

Before storms, horses are nervous and are more apt to bolt. Lambs and calves romp and frolic, kicking up their heels in the wind. Perhaps you have felt this urge to run about the yard just before a storm strikes. Any experienced teacher will tell you that children are rowdier before a storm. Old farmers say the following are sure signs of rain, and they made rhymes to make them easier to remember:

Watch the heifer's tail;
When stretched aloft, 'twill rain or hail.

'Twill rain when rams and lambkins are full of play,
And butt at each other's heads in mimic fray.

When a cow tries to scratch her ear,
It means a shower is near.

A cow might be scratching her ear because it is ringing. On the other hand, she might be scratching it because she has a tick. It is always a good idea to find two or more signs before making a prediction.

Some other old sayings along this line are:

When the donkey begins to bray,
Be sure we shall have rain that day.

When a rooster crows at noon,
Rain will come soon.

A cow *may* scratch her ear because it will rain soon.

When a cow bellows three times without stopping,
A storm will come hopping.

These animals might be making a fuss because they are uncomfortable, but on the other hand they might just have something else on their minds. If you notice all these signs at the same time, it probably means that the animals are uncomfortable. But if there is just one of them, look for more signs of pressure drop. If it is a valid sign, you will always be able to find more.

Three

Creepy Creatures and Other Wildlife

You can find many weather signs among wildlife, because of their highly developed senses. Pressure drops affect small mammals and insects in many ways. Try looking in or near the house. Mice and cockroaches are good weather indicators. Outdoorsmen have observed that field mice run out of their holes and squeak and frolic before a storm.

One old grandmother recalls lying in bed as a child listening to the mice playing endless games of tag along the rafters overhead.

When her mother heard them, she always closed the window, saying, "Rain's coming when mice dance on the sill, and their voice is loud and shrill."

"They sounded as if they were having such fun," said the old lady, "squealing and frolicking like girls at a

Field mice often scamper around before a storm.

slumber party. Then the storm would blow in and put an end to their enjoyment."

Another bit of folklore that seems to be fairly valid is: "When cockroaches fly, rain will drop by."

Cockroaches become more active before a storm.

A drop in air pressure probably produces this behavior, but it might also be caused by infrasound. In-
frasounds are natural sounds so low in pitch that the
human ear cannot detect them. Scientists have learned
that before many natural disasters, such as severe
storms, tornadoes, earthquakes, and volcanoes, in-
frasonic sounds are given off, which can be heard with
sensitive microphones. It is believed that some animals
may also be able to hear them. Dr. Ruth Simon, a
member of a United States geological team, has been
using cockroaches in an experiment to detect oncoming
earthquakes in California. She has found that even before an earthquake of the smallest intensity, the roaches
become more active. University of California at Los
Angeles scientists are using mice and kangaroo rats in a
similar experiment. Perhaps the weather-wise American who scorns leeches and frogs in jars will keep boxes
of cockroaches or mice instead, to help predict storms
and other natural disasters!

Those to whom this does not appeal could watch
wild ground creatures. Besides seeking shelter before a
storm, they indicate pressure drops in other ways.

When you see a sandy beach come alive with large
numbers of sea crabs, it is time to pick up your beach
gear and head for shelter. A change in air pressure over
the water warns the crabs that a storm is coming.
Rather than take the beating of a stormy sea pounding
the shore, they leave the water and seek shelter on land.

Bats protest loudly and will sometimes even try to
fly into the house under low-pressure conditions. Even
fish know when it is time to take shelter. Ewart Autry

tells this story in the September 1959 issue of *Farm Journal:*

"One day a friend and I were catching crappies at a depth of about three feet.

"But suddenly they stopped biting. My friend let his line down to six feet and immediately got a strike. I lowered my line and also got a strike.

" 'We'd better get out of here,' said my companion. 'When fish suddenly go deeper, there's a storm brewing.'

"We barely made it to the highway when the downpour started."

Almost any farm boy can tell you that he catches more rabbits in his box traps just before a thunderstorm or heavy snow. Some believe this is because animals have an instinct to eat more before storms. But the rabbits could be seeking a safe shelter. To them the box trap probably looks like a hollow log. It is well known that rabbits leave the open fields and head for the woods before a storm.

Squirrels sometimes become quarrelsome and scrappy with one another. Or they may be extra frisky, frolicking around and playing boisterous games of follow-the-leader all morning long, up one tree, down the next, and leaping great distances just before a storm strikes. And when you see the females busily patching up and reinforcing their nests, it is time for you to seek some kind of shelter for yourself. You can be sure of a hard downpour soon.

Woodsmen have reported seeing female opossums and raccoons carrying their young away from their hollow log homes on a creek bank just before a flooding rain. How did they know the creek would overflow? Maybe they sensed the change in air pressure and from past experience knew it meant danger.

Deer leave the high ground and come down from the mountains before a storm. If you see this, you can be sure that a storm will strike within two days.

A hunter relates this story:

"One fall some friends and I were hunting deer in a little valley in Colorado. We hadn't seen a single deer. Then on the third day we noticed all the deer tracks led downhill toward a thickly forested area lower down the mountain. Realizing what that meant, we got out of there as quickly as we could. That night a heavy snow closed the valley for the winter."

Out west, old range riders say they know they are going to have a blizzard when the coyotes move in close to their camps and stay around day and night.

Birds also seek shelter before a storm. You will sometimes see birds roosting in pine and cedar trees or huddling together on a wire close to a building during the daytime. This is a good storm signal. Pre-storm low pressure makes the air so thin that birds have difficulty flying, so they go to roost. Thus we have:

> When birds stop singing
> And trees start swinging,
> A storm is on its way.
>
> Robin's in the bush
> Rain will come with a rush.

If you see a robin enter a barn, expect a heavy downpour.

Seabirds sit out a storm on land. Anytime you see sea gulls or other seabirds sitting on the ground in large clusters, reluctant to fly, it is not a very good day to go sailing. Remember this old sailor's warning:

Sea gull, sea gull, sitting on the sand;
It's never good weather while you're on land.

On the other hand, Maine fishermen say,

Wild geese, wild geese going out to sea
All fine weather it will be.

It is unusual to see large flocks of birds flying over in the summertime, rather than during the periods of

Sea gulls stay on land before and during storms.

migration in the spring or fall. Watch for other weather signs if you see this. You should also stay alert if you see migrating birds flying in the wrong direction. These birds may be flying ahead of a storm.

And if you can't see a bird anywhere, look out! They may have flown to a region not affected by an approaching violent storm.

Ewart Autry also told this story in his *Farm Journal* article:

> One day a storm began to gather in the west at noon. The sky grew dark and threatening. The usual congregation of buzzards was in the trees and pasture along the river.
>
> They had stayed there through many rains before, but this time, they arose suddenly and went southward with a furious flapping of wings as if speed was very important.
>
> Twenty minutes later a terrific hail storm broke in fury. Hailstones as large as hen eggs pounded through roofs and battered the crops. It covered many miles eastward, westward and northward, but only three miles southward!
>
> The Weather Bureau had forecast a partly cloudy day, and none of our local prophets had foreseen hail. But those lowly turkey buzzards knew.

Birds and bats have very sensitive ears and feel the change in air pressure more keenly than people do. Pre-storm air-pressure drops are very painful to them. Then too, they fly above the earth and can detect pressure changes sooner than ground animals. It is also possible the buzzards in this case heard the infrasound generated by the storm system that produced the hail.

Birds are especially good weather indicators because they show the effect of a pressure drop in many ways. Some birds become irritable and quarrelsome and will squabble over a piece of bread crust. Flocks of sparrows chirp like a roomful of children chattering all at once. Other birds sing until they nearly burst their throats just before a storm. It seems they know they won't get another chance for an hour or two. People say that robins give a "rain hollering." They may be warning other creatures who haven't yet noticed the change in pressure. Another saying is, "If a crow hollers in the morning, expect rain by night." The Zuni Indians say, "When chimney swifts circle and call, they speak of rain."

Most birds prefer to feed early in the morning. But before a storm, especially a snowstorm, you can often see many wild birds feeding late in the day. Sometimes large flocks of starlings cover a lawn, like a black blanket, and greedily peck away until nearly dark. Many birds will eat heavier just before a rain, cleaning out a bird feeder in half the time they usually take.

Of course, if you are observing birds at a feeder you must consider when food was put out. If it was put out late in the day, birds eating late would not necessarily indicate an approaching storm. Also, you should consider the habits of different species. Some of them may prefer to feed late.

Migrating birds use air-pressure changes to find columns of rising warm air, called thermal updrafts. Thermal updrafts lift birds to great heights, the same way hot-air lifts a balloon. Ducks and geese can rest their wings in an updraft without landing. Hawks use updrafts as an elevator. When you see hawks flying straight up, you can expect afternoon showers, because the air pressure is changing.

You may have seen birds flying in an unusual or erratic way, soaring and dipping as if they were a bit tipsy or on a roller coaster. Such unusual flying may be caused by unstable air or changing air conditions with strong thermal updrafts. This unstable air usually brings afternoon showers. Erratic flying can also be an indication of thin upper air caused by a drop in air pressure. Birds have to beat their wings harder and faster to stay up when the air is thin.

Have you ever seen birds flying so low that their wings nearly touch the ground? This is also an indica-

Birds fly low when the air pressure drops.

tion of a sudden air-pressure drop. They are flying near
the ground because the air pressure is higher there.
Thus the old rhyme:

> Birds flying high;
> The weather will be dry.
> Birds flying near the ground;
> Soon you'll hear the thunder's sound.

Bats, swallows, chimney swifts, mockingbirds,
purple martins, and many other kinds of birds may be
flying low for another reason. They feed in flight on
flying insects. On hot, dry days, insects are carried high
by rising hot air. Birds fly high to find their prey. When
air pressure drops, insects are carried downward as the
heavier, cool air sinks to the ground. The insects may
not be as easy to see as the birds and bats that are
darting low to feed on them. However, almost everyone
is familiar with the swarms of gnats that fly almost at
face level on hot, humid days.

There is one thing you should remember. Although
many of these old sayings claim to be signs of rain, it
would be more accurate to say they are signs of falling
air pressure. Sometimes it does not rain even though
the air pressure drops very low. Although pressure
always falls before a rain, it does not always rain when
the pressure drops. There must also be a high moisture
content in the air. It is usually the combination of high
humidity (moisture) and a pressure drop that affects
plants and animals and causes the behavior we read as
weather signs.

Four

Signs of Humidity
in Nature

Many things in nature make good humidity indicators. Spiders are among the best. Two city families learned this the hard way while spending a weekend on a lake in southern Missouri. Jones lost a coin toss for the best campsite and pitched his tent on a level spot nearer the water. It was low, but he felt safe. They were only staying two nights, and the Weather Bureau's five-day forecast had predicted fair weather.

After supper they sat around chatting with an old-man who had dropped by and who told them where to find the best fishing spots. They began discussing a rising time so they could get an early start in the morning.

"You might get up earlier than you expect," the old-timer drawled.

41

"Why?" the campers asked.

"Likely to be a real gully washer before morning. Water will run right through that tent." He pointed to the Jones's tent.

"What makes you think it will rain?" demanded Jones. "There's not a cloud in the sky."

"That spider," replied the old man, pointing to a big brown spider who was busily taking down her web from a tree limb overhead. "Spiders don't do that unless there is going to be a heavy rain."

Everyone laughed, but the old man and the spider got the last laugh when the Jones family was awakened around three A.M. by rain pounding on their tent and water streaming through it.

The man's prediction was more accurate than the official weather forecast because he knew the way of

Spiders take in their nets just before a heavy rainstorm.

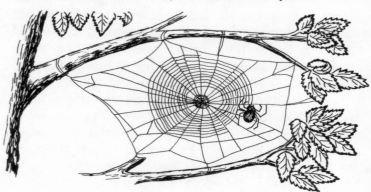

spiders, and the spider knew the conditions right there at that moment; the weather was humid and the pressure was dropping.

You can bet the Jones family will not forget that:

> When spiders take in their net,
> The ground will soon be wet.

Meteorologists tell us that during fair weather the air usually contains very little moisture. But just before a rain the air becomes humid and has a higher relative humidity. Humidity is the amount of moisture (water vapor) in the air. Relative humidity is the amount of moisture in the air compared to how much it could hold. When the air has all the moisture it can hold, it is saturated. You might compare it to a sponge. When a sponge is damp it is wet, but has relatively little moisture in it. When it is dripping wet, it is saturated. When air is cooled it cannot hold as much moisture as when it is warm. If air is cooled to its saturation point, the moisture will condense and fall as rain. You have seen drops of water on the outside of a glass of ice water. This happens because the warm, moist room air touching the glass has been cooled to the saturation point.

Meteorologists use a hygrometer to measure relative humidity. Before the invention of the hygrometer people relied on nature to tell them when the humidity was high. And spiders could be relied upon to do a pretty good job of this.

Normally, spiders spin their webs between 6 and 7 P.M. During calm, clear weather they don't bother to make large webs or to take them in. But when there is

high humidity and a drop in air pressure, spiders work
overtime building more and larger dragnets. Somehow
they seem to know that insects will be easier to catch
when the humidity is high. Moisture soaks the insects'
wings, making it difficult for them to fly. However,
since a heavy rain would ruin the net and wash away the
bugs caught in it, spiders will take down their nets
before a storm.

> When insects fly low,
> Rain comes, yet not slow.

When you see spiders working feverishly spinning
huge webs late into the evening, you can be sure the
humidity is high. Have you ever walked in the woods a
few hours before a rain and run into a great number of
webs stretched across your path? All of them seem to
be at face level!

According to an old Indian saying, "Spiders en-
large their traps before bad weather," and "Tarantulas
crawl in the daytime, rain will surely come."

Insects are most active about twelve hours before a
storm. They stop flying two hours before the rain starts.
Many spiders take advantage of this increased activity,
then pull in their webs just before the storm strikes,
unless they are indoors. In that case there is another
proverb:

> When spiders cease to expand their webs,
> Look for clearing weather.

A story is told about a French general who had

been thrown into prison because he had lost a campaign in the rain-soaked bogs of Prussia during the Franco-Prussian War. Having nothing better to do all day, he watched the spiders spinning their webs in the corners of his cell. One day he noticed that they had "ceased to expand their webs." Positive it meant the weather would clear, he talked his superiors into releasing him and allowing him to launch another battle against the Prussians. They did, and he went on to victory over the then-frozen bogs.

Farmers have a proverb about spiders and their webs:

> If spiders their webs forsake,
> The weather for certain will break.

Spiders seem to know when the rain is over, and take a rest from their spinning, feeding upon what they caught during the rainy spell.

You can also rejoice and safely plan an all-day outing when you see cobwebs on the grass. There are, of course, cobwebs on the grass most any time, but you seldom see them unless they are covered with dew. Dew only forms when the sky is clear and there is no wind. Under these conditions the barometric pressure is usually high and fair weather is ahead for the next twenty-four hours at least. Dew forms when the earth cools after sundown, causing the air near the ground to cool below the dew point. The moisture in the air condenses onto the grass and cobwebs.

When the sky is covered with clouds, the earth does not cool enough to cause condensation of moisture. In the past people were so sure of this sign that generals used it to decide if the day would be clear enough to fight a battle.

> When dew is on the grass,
> Rain will never come to pass.

And the reverse:

> When grass is dry at morning light,
> look for rain before the night.

The most usual cause for a lack of dew is a cloudy sky and wind, both conditions that bring rain. However, even if the sky is clear and there is no wind, dew will not form when the air is very dry or when the ground air does not cool to the dew point. This sometimes happens during very hot, dry periods. Therefore, this proverb is not always reliable. Check other conditions.

Many animals take advantage of the effect of high humidity on insects. Frogs and toads come out and feast on the easily caught insects when the air is cool and moist.

"If toads come out of their holes in great numbers, rain will fall soon," is an old saying of farmers.

Toads seldom come out when the air is dry. This is also true of frogs, and is another reason you can hear more of them before a rain.

Sometimes you see many snails crawling in flower beds or along a wall. Snails live in dark, damp places, under rocks, dead logs, or leaves. When the air is

Frogs can catch many insects when the air is humid.

humid, they come out to look for food. Farmers say:

> When black snails on the road you see,
> Then on the morrow rain will be.

Fish also take advantage of low-flying insects. When you see large numbers of fish leaping out of the water for insects skimming just above the surface, you can bet the air is very humid, and the air pressure low.

> Before a rain the fishes rise
> And nimbly catch incautious flies.

The fish probably sense the change in atmospheric

Fish can easily catch bugs when insects fly low during periods of high humidity and low air pressure.

pressure on the water and know insects will be closer to the surface and easier to catch.

Avid fishermen say that fish refuse to take a lure before a storm. They most likely have already eaten their fill. This is another bit of fisherman's weather lore:

> When trout refuse bait or fly,
> There is a storm nearby.

Farmers say that fleas, flies, and gnats bite harder and cling tighter just before rain. They recite this rhyme:

> The gnats bite and I scratch in vain,
> Because they know it is going to rain.

Perhaps you have noticed that fleas bite harder after a dog has had a bath. This is probably because the dog's skin is moist. Some people also think that it is because people and animals sweat more when the air is very humid, and flies and fleas are attracted by that. Whatever it is, according to farmers, it is a reliable sign.

When it is humid, cows swat at the flies with their tails. The harder the flies bite, the harder and more often the cows swat, which led to the saying:

> If the cow thumps her ribs with her tail,
> Be prepared for rain or hail.

Has your mother ever said, "Close the door, you are letting the flies in?" Or have you ever been awakened in the morning by a pesky fly who insists upon landing on your nose? Everytime you shoo it off, it comes right back. Flies, spiders, ants, and many other kinds of insects will enter or try to enter your house just before a storm. On some days it seems as if every time you open the door, three or four flies come in. This is a good indication of very humid air and, more often than not, means a long, heavy rain.

> A fly on your nose
> You swat and it goes,
> If it comes back again,
> It will bring a good rain.

Some people watch ants for weather clues. Once a group of Texas teenagers were backpacking alongside a stream in a narrow gorge. They had barely unpacked everything for a quick lunch when one of the members noticed some big black ants frantically building up the walls around their nest.

"We'd better get out of here," he said.

"Why?" the others wanted to know.

"My grandfather says when ants do that they are preparing for a heavy rain. I wouldn't want to get caught here when it comes."

They set a record packing up and barely made it out of the gorge before the downpour began.

Anytime you see ants industriously building huge mounds around their holes, prepare for rain. About two hours before a downpour, all kinds of ants, but especially large black or red ants, will break up their caravans, scurry into their nests, and begin building dams around the ant hills. These mounds, which are sometimes several inches in height, prevent rainwater from

Ants build dams around ant hills to keep them from being flooded when rain threatens.

running into the ant hills. The ants will stay inside until the rain is over. Remember this verse:

When ants build high,
Rain will fall from the sky.

Ants carrying eggs can be a reliable weather indicator, if you are familiar with the colony and can be sure they are carrying their own and are not stealing eggs from another ant nest.

Theophrastus wrote, "If ants on the side of a hollow carry their eggs from the nest to high ground, it indicates rain."

Someone else put it into rhyme:

When ants move their eggs and climb,
Rain is coming anytime.

Ants often bring their eggs out into the warm sun to speed up their hatching. When you see them in a great hurry to get the eggs back inside, you can expect a storm.

Some people say an open ant hole indicates clear weather, a closed one an approaching storm. Some ants do close their holes before a storm. But they also close them when they expect a raid by another colony of ants. So you can't rely on this one for a storm warning. However, an open hole is a good fair-weather sign.

Bees give weather clues, too. They are unusually active several hours before a rain. As the humidity increases, they return to their hives. When their activity stops and the bees stay near home, you can expect a rain in about two hours. Some American Indians say that the longer the increased activity lasts, the longer the rain will be. Farmers say:

> If bees stay at home,
> Rain will soon come.
> If they fly away,
> Fine will be the day.

> When bees to distance wing their flight,
> Days are warm and skies are bright.
> But when their flight ends near their home,
> Stormy weather is sure to come.

So keep an eye out for a beehive.

Butterflies usually flit from flower to flower all day long. When they suddenly disappear and can be found hiding on tree trunks or on the undersides of leaves, you can be sure they are seeking shelter to protect their fragile wings from a hard rain.

Most of the time sow bugs (wood lice) are found in cool, damp places, under rocks or rotten logs. But when the air is very humid they can be found on sidewalks, driveways, and other open places.

Glowworms, the females of some species of fireflies, like sow bugs, live underground or in rotted wood and leaves. When the air is humid, they also come out to feed upon other small insects. The damper the air, the more glowworms you will see. Therefore:

> When the glowworm lights her lamp,
> The air is always damp.

Fireflies fly very low when there is a high relative humidity. But an old saying states, "When fireflies are about in large numbers, the weather will be fair for the next three days."

In addition, if you hear lots of locusts singing, you can be sure the air is dry. Locusts sing only when it is hot and dry.

It is easy to understand why Benjamin Franklin said, "One little bug knows more about rain than all the almanacs."

If you are alert and keep your eyes and ears open, you will find more ways that insects and animals react to high humidity. Listen to the insects' chirping. Is it especially loud? Are the insects more numerous? Are they found in unusual places?

And how about yourself? How does humidity affect you?

Five

Humidity and You

Some people are very sensitive to humidity. People who have arthritis are, in a sense, "living hygrometers." High humidity causes the fluid in their tissues and joints to increase, making movement difficult and painful. That is why many older people say, "It's going to rain, I can feel it in my bones." They actually can.

New Englanders used to call cold, damp weather "horse-chestnut weather." There was an old superstition that if you carried a horse chestnut in your pocket you wouldn't get rheumatism.

Humidity affects some people in another way. Researchers have found that as humidity rises, so do crimes of violence, suicides, and vandalism. Therefore, when you get an urge to tear something up, take a good look outside for the reason. Then turn your urge to something creative, like weather forecasting.

American Indians knew their braves would be excitable and irritable just before a storm, so they planned their war parties and raids during those times. They claimed: "Storm gods give courage to red man."

Almost everyone knows what humidity does to hair. Curly hair gets curlier and straight hair gets limp. Thus we have this old weather proverb:

> Curls that kink and cords that bind:
> Signs of rain and heavy wind.

The reason, of course, is that hair absorbs moisture from damp air. Straight hair actually gets longer. A Swiss geologist used this fact to invent the first hygrometer. In 1783 Horace Bénédict de Saussure fastened some human hair to a needle. The hair expanded when the air was moist, and contracted when the air was dry, moving the needle across a numbered scale. His instrument is called a hair hygrometer and is still used by meteorologists. They say a child's hair works best, and that blond hair is better than brunet for this purpose.

Your senses of smell, hearing, and sight give good weather clues, too. Jimmy Cross learned to trust his sense of smell one day. When he and his father went out to the car, Mr. Cross detected the strong, pungent fumes of escaping gasoline. He checked the cap on the gas tank, then looked under the car for a leak or wet spot. But he didn't find anything.

Jimmy noticed that their elderly neighbor's roses were unusually fragrant.

"That's because it is going to rain," declared their neighbor.

"It can't!" protested Jimmy. "We're on our way to the ball game. Besides, the weatherman said it wouldn't."

"Spot thinks it will." The old man pointed to Jimmy's dog, who was running around the yard sniffing the air.

His weather-wise neighbor had saved him from a soaking more than once, so Jimmy got his raincoat. Sure enough, it began to rain during the seventh inning, and they were the only ones in the ball park with raincoats.

Many people know from long experience that when odors hang heavier than usual in the air, rain follows. The sweet, heavy odor of flowers is much more apparent when air is humid. Often people say, "It smells like rain."

If humans, with their poorly developed sense of smell, notice the difference, then it shouldn't be surprising to learn that other animals do too. Many of us have observed dogs and horses stretching their necks and sniffing the air just before a shower. They might be able to smell the rain, or they could be sniffing the many unusual odors released by a lowering air pressure.

> Dogs or horses sniffing the air;
> A summer shower will soon be there.

Dogs are able to track game much better when the pressure is low. Everything smells stronger, from cooking odors to the musky smell of a skunk.

Although people can't smell as well as animals,

Dog sniffing the air before a shower.

they become aware of odors they don't normally smell, such as strong gasoline fumes from an automobile or boat motor. Have you ever noticed that sometimes the decaying vegetation around ponds, ditches, or swamps smells rotten and at other times you don't notice it at all? Heavy high-pressure air holds many odors in so they can't be detected. Low pressure allows trapped gases from decayed vegetation to escape. Swamps and clam beds look like slowly boiling pots of mud as the gases rise. Thus we have this old saying:

> When ditch and pond offend the nose,
> Then look for rain and stormy blows.

Sometimes great amounts of marsh gases are released by low air pressure. Moonlight shining on this escaping gas is an eerie sight. People often travel many miles to see it.

Your sense of sound is keener when the air is damp. Sounds seem nearer and clearer just before a rain. Sometimes you can hear church bells, factory or train whistles, or boat horns that are five to ten miles away. Sounds do not usually travel that distance. When this happens, you can be sure the air is very humid. Sound waves travel better in damp air than in dry air. Voices can be heard plainly a half mile away in a fog. Clouds also help. They bounce the sound waves back to earth, giving an echo effect. In fair weather sound waves spread out into space and become lost. People noticed this a very long time ago. Elijah is quoted in the Old Testament as saying, "There is a sound of rushing of rain" (I Kings 18:41). Today we are more familiar with these sayings:

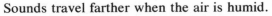

Sounds travel farther when the air is humid.

> When sounds are clear,
> Rain is near.

Or, as the English say:

> Sound traveling far and wide
> A stormy day will betide.

Sailors say,

> When boat horns sound hollow,
> Rain will surely follow.

You can also see farther when the air is very humid because light rays carry better in humid air. Many land-lubbers taking their first boat to the seashore are mis-led by a clear, crisp sky and faraway objects that look sharp and distinct.

What a wonderful weekend for sailing, they think. Little do they realize that under such conditions it will most certainly storm within twenty-four hours!

Distant hills or shorelines usually look dim and gray. When the air pressure is high and there is little wind, dust particles in the air reduce the distance one can see and make objects look fuzzy. Near the ocean the evaporation of salt water causes a haze that dims the sharp line of the horizon. When a low-pressure system moves in, the hills or shorelines become very clear and seem closer. That is because unstable air and wind accompanying the low blow away the dust and haze.

The way you see colors can change with weather conditions. Two boys learned this while Scuba diving at

Sailors say, "The farther the sight, the nearer the rain."

their favorite lake with an older friend. It was mid-afternoon when they arrived. The water, which was usually green or a light glassy blue, had a strange, greasy, slate-gray look.

"I think I'll stay up here and watch awhile," their older friend said.

"Why? What's the matter?" the boys asked.

"My instructor always told me to be wary of slate-gray water. It could mean the barometer is falling. Sometimes thundershowers form awfully quickly."

The weather report that morning had been for scattered showers.

"You fellows go ahead and dive if you wish, but better not go too deep. Check back with me in about fifteen minutes, okay?"

The boys agreed, and later they all had to run to

their car, where they sat out a brief but severe thunderstorm.

Tricky local weather conditions can arise in a few minutes. Therefore, all of the local conditions you can find should be noted and carefully evaluated. Again, remember that although many of the weather adages given here say they are signs of rain or storm, they actually indicate high humidity and sometimes a drop in air pressure. Where these two conditions exist together, rain or storms are likely, but high humidity by itself will not cause rain any more than low pressure will.

Six

Other Signs of Humidity

Have you ever awakened in the morning and found a "fairy ring" of toadstools where none existed the night before? Seeing one of these rings makes it easy to believe in elves and fairies! You may have been so thrilled with the discovery of it that you never stopped to realize why the toadstools were there. In reality the spores were there all along, just waiting for a very humid night to make them pop up out of the ground. Thus we have this weather verse:

> If toadstools you see in the morning,
> Expect much rain before evening.

Actually, when mushrooms appear in the morning, they indicate that a very damp evening has passed. You

63

A "fairy ring" of toadstools.

will never see a toadstool unless the air has almost reached the saturation point. Sometimes this happens before a rain, or after a long rainy spell or dense fog.

Plants are handy humidity indicators. There are nearly always some around when you need them. Humidity affects plants in different ways. The sensitive plant closes its leaves when the air is damp. Many flowers close their blossoms just before a rain. Weather watchers have called the scarlet pimpernel the "poor man's barometer" because its flowers open only in fair weather. This weather verse, or one similar to it, is known around the world:

> Pimpernel, pimpernel, tell me true
> Whether the weather be fine or no.

Many other flowers also close their blossoms.

Mushrooms grow well in humid weather.
Courtesy Alice Gilbreath

Among the more common ones are the yellow anemone, daisy, morning glory, gentian, dandelion, and tulip.

Botanists (people who study plants) say that the plants oᶠ the bean family react to weather changes by cupping up their leaves whenever the sky is heavily overcast. Farmers say, "When the down of the dandelion closes up, it is a sign of rain."

Clover plants draw their leaves together before a rain; pine cones open in dry weather and close in humid; milkweeds close up when the humidity is high.

Of all plants, the effect of high humidity is easiest to see on the silver maple and cottonwood trees. About twenty-four hours before the rain starts these trees begin turning over their leaves. All hardwood trees turn over their leaves before a rain, but it is easier to see on these two types because the undersides of their leaves are silver, so there is a greater contrast in the color of the two sides. It almost looks like magic when the whole tree changes from deep green to silver.

It is believed that the absorption of moisture from the air causes a change in the leaf stalk, making the leaves turn over. It may be that the rough underside of the leaf can absorb rain better than the smooth topside.

Other trees show the underside of their leaves when the wind shifts just before the rain starts. Thermal updrafts can also cause leaves to flip over. In this case the leaves quiver.

> When leaves show their undersides,
> Be very sure that rain betides.

Campers might be surprised to learn that their campfires are good weather indicators. Long ago when people cooked outside almost all of the time, they discovered that fires burn more vigorously just before bad weather. This is because the lowering air pressure causes more wind, which gives the fire more oxygen.

On fair days the smoke rises straight up into the sky or drifts gently off in one direction. If a storm is approaching, the smoke will curl downward and linger, hugging the ground. Pre-storm air has low pressure, making it lighter than smoke, and high humidity. The moisture in the air condenses onto the smoke particles, increasing smoke's weight. Any low-lying clouds act as a blanket and prevent smoke from rising. People would say:

The moisture in prestorm air condenses into smoke parti-cles, preventing the smoke from rising.

'Twill rain when smoke from chimney ascends
Then curling back, to earth, it bends.

Or more simply:

When smoke is sluggish in rising,
Be prepared for wet weather.

Fishermen who think fish bite best just before a rain say:

When smoke curls down and ditches reek,
The wise angler heads straight for the creek.

A fireplace can give you still another clue to a weather change. Watch for bits of black soot that have fallen down into a thoroughly cleaned fireplace. Soot is very light. Most of the time, when the air is dry, it sticks to the chimney walls. When the air is very humid, some of the moisture condenses onto the soot, which becomes damp and relatively heavy. If a drop in air pressure causes a downdraft in the chimney, the heavier soot breaks off and falls into the fireplace. High humidity can also affect the way firewood burns. Firewood crackles when it has absorbed moisture from very humid air.

Many things in and around your home absorb moisture in this way. Most people, like Jane Sowers, think of them as annoyances rather than humidity indicators. Jane stumbled across the room to shut the window one morning, but it stuck and refused to close. Feeling cross and grumpy, she bent down to get a pair of socks from her dresser drawer. It, too, stuck. With a mighty tug, she pulled it loose so suddenly that she landed ker-plop on the floor, with the drawer's contents on top of her. The knot in her shoestring refused to be untied. Her hair frizzed and kinked and would not comb down neatly. When she tried to salt her egg at breakfast, the salt wouldn't come out of the shaker. Then she was caught in the rain on the way to school. The last need not have happened. She had had plenty of warning.

Almost everyone is familiar with lumpy table salt that sticks together and will not shake out. If the air is very damp, there may be drops of water on the salt shaker's lid. Some things just feel damp when they absorb moisture. Others, like the wood in windows and dresser drawers, swell. Absorbed moisture makes them fit tighter so that they are hard to open or close. Knots

Drawers expand and stick when the air is moist.

in shoestrings and ropes are difficult to untie, because they, too, become swollen when they absorb moisture.

Many people in coastal areas keep a strip of seaweed in the house as a humidity indicator. They say if the seaweed stays dry and dusty, the weather will be fair. If moisture from the air makes it damp and sticky, rain is on the way. Moss can be used in the same way.

>Seaweed dry, sunny sky;
>Seaweed wet, rain you'll get.

Walls, pavement, and stones do not absorb moisture, but they "sweat." When warm, moist air strikes the cool surface of a brick wall, a sidewalk, or a stone, moisture condenses on it, causing it to feel damp. If other signs show a drop in pressure, this is usually a good indication of rain. Remember:

> When stones sweat,
> Rain you'll get.

No one needs to be told that the humidity is very high during a fog. Although there may be less than a gallon of water in a cubic mile of air, it is almost saturated. A fog forms when the ground air is cooled to near the saturation point (dew point).

> A summer fog for fair;
> A winter fog for rain.

New Englanders say:

> Fog from seaward, fair weather;
> Fog from landward, rain.

Summer fogs are formed when hot air cools to the dew point on windless, cloudless nights. They usually burn off before noon. Winter fogs are formed when warm, moist air is moved in over cold land surfaces by a low-pressure system, and they are either followed by rain, or remain for several days. Thus:

> Evening fog will not burn soon;
> Morning fog will burn 'fore noon.

Sometimes it is helpful to know if the humidity is low, not only because low humidity means fair weather, but because of the great danger of forest and range fires when the air is very dry. This proverb tells you one way to find out:

If you see sparks when you stroke a cat's back,
The weather will be fair.

The sparks tell you the air is very dry. Static electricity does not build up in humid air.

There are other conditions besides weather changes that can cause high humidity. It is normally damp and humid along a seacoast, lakeshore, or a large river. It will also be very humid after a long rainy spell, even though the air pressure is rising. Rising air pressure should indicate clearing and fair weather. Remember, you must know what is normal for the place where you are. Keep in mind that the unusual things in nature are the good weather signs. However, what may be a very good sign of a weather change in one area may not work at all in another. Look for other weather elements that will give you more clues to weather changes, such as temperature and wind.

Seven

Temperature and Weather

On almost any hot summer day you can hear someone ask, "Is it hot enough for you?" or on a very cold wintry day, "Is it cold enough for you?" The only time many people think about temperature in connection with weather is when it is either too hot or too cold to suit them.

But temperature is a very important part of weather. It must be taken into account in making predictions. Nothing in nature happens all by itself. Everything is interwoven and fits together like a giant jigsaw puzzle. Air pressure, humidity, temperature, and wind all have something to do with each other and work together to make up weather.

When the temperature of the air changes, so does the barometric pressure. Temperature changes cause

73

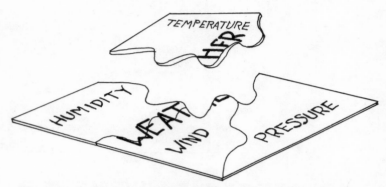

Weather is like a giant jigsaw puzzle, made up of many different parts.

wind and they also affect the amount of moisture in the air. The higher the temperature, the more water vapor air can hold. If the temperature of the air becomes cool enough, the water vapor in it condenses onto particles of dust and forms clouds. When the air becomes cooler still, it rains or snows. If the temperature of the air never changed at all, we would not have any weather changes.

Nature most often cools air by raising it to cooler altitudes. If you have ever climbed a mountain you know the air on top is much cooler than the air in the valley. That is because air cools 5½ degrees for every thousand feet it rises. Sometimes warm air is forced up over a hill or mountain. If it is forced to rise high enough, and if the air is very humid, the colder temperatures existing at the higher altitude will cause the humidity to condense, forming rain. This rain will fall on the windward side of the mountain, because air stops cooling after it passes over the top. Air also rises by convection, that is, it gets warm, expands, and rises. This results in local thunderstorms. But air is most often cooled by being forced upward over a wedge of cooler air. That is what produces most of the rain or snow that falls.

The temperature of the air usually drops at night, too. If the air is dry, the temperature will drop relatively low because heat radiates easily through dry air. Then the water vapor will condense onto grass, forming dew, and a fair day will follow. If the air is very humid, the drop will be small, because moist air absorbs much of the sun's heat by day and prevents loss of heat from the earth's surface at night. It could rain the next day. Rain

Three ways nature cools air.

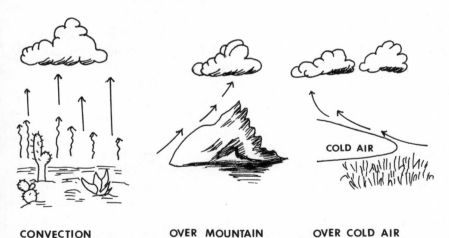

CONVECTION   OVER MOUNTAIN   OVER COLD AIR

is almost a certainty if the temperature rises during the night. Indians in New England say:

> When the night has a fever,
> It cries in the morning.

For the temperature to rise at night, the air would have to be very humid with a warm wind from the south or southeast. The pressure would be falling and there would probably be a cloud cover.

Meteorologists use thermometers to measure temperature. The first thermometer, invented in 1593 by Galileo, was not like the thermometers of today. It was a large bulb filled with air, which forced the water level in a tube downward when heated. Later, in 1612, Galileo made an alcohol thermometer that was very much like those in use today.

Meteorologists use temperature readings to draw up forecasts. They tell us that the temperature often rises just before a storm. You know if the day is hot or cold, but you cannot know the exact change in temperature without a thermometer. However, during the summertime, there are clues to rising temperatures.

It has long been known that temperature affects people. In the middle ages, a killer was not executed if he could prove he committed the murder during the foehn (a hot dry wind that raised the temperature as much as 40° F). Modern studies have proved that during long periods of very hot weather people become irritable. Tempers flare and antisocial behavior increases. Police department records show that as the days get hotter, crime increases. More riots occur during the hot dry days of July and August than any other part of the year. However, after the temperature reaches 90 to 95 degrees, crimes begin to decrease, because extreme heat saps energy. Therefore, if everyone becomes listless after being irritable, you have a clue that the temperature has risen above 95 degrees.

Temperature also affects the behavior of animals. The hot, dry days of July and August are sometimes called "dog days." Many people associate this name with dogs, because they become irritable and it was thought that they go mad more often during hot spells. However, the term "dog days" actually is derived from ancient Roman times and refers to the rising of the Dog Star, Sirius.

Long ago people cooked on wood stoves or on open fires outdoors. In summer their houses were very hot, so they were much more aware of temperature changes than we are. They noticed that many insects were affected by temperature changes. Modern scientists have studied the effect of heat upon insects and have confirmed what the ancients said.

Temperature affects the way a black cricket chirps. As the temperature rises, the cricket chirps more rapidly. If you count the number of chirps the cricket makes in fourteen seconds and add the number you get to forty, you will have the temperature in Fahrenheit degrees. This will be accurate to within one or two degrees. You can get a still more accurate reading by making three or more counts. Find the average number of chirps for the three counts, then add that number to 40. It will help to have a companion count off the seconds while you count the chirps. If you counted

Crickets chirp more when it is hot.

38 chirps the first time, 37 the second time, and 39 the third time, the average would be 38 chirps. 38 added to 40 is 78. The temperature where the cricket is sitting is 78° F.

Katydids are also sensitive to temperature changes. Scientists have learned that you can get an approximate temperature reading by listening to the length of their call. When the temperature is above 78° F., katydids give their full call, "Kay-tee-did-it." At approximately 74° F. their call is shortened to "Kay-tee-didn't." At about 70° F. it is shorter still, "Kay-tee-did." At around 66° F. it is "Kate didn't," at 62° F., "Kate-tee." At 58° F. it is simply "Kate," and at 55° F. or lower, katydids are silent.

Bees can also give a clue to temperature, because flowers act a little like thermometers. The warmer the

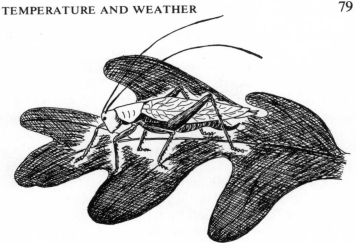

The call of a katydid gets shorter as the temperature drops.

air is, the more nectar the flower has. Therefore, the warmer it is, up to a point, the more active the bees are. But if the sky is clear and you can see no bees at all in places where you normally see many, then the temperature is probably above 102° F. Bees stay in or near the hive in such high temperatures.

On the other hand, if no ants visited your picnic table on a cool, clear day, then the temperature was probably below 54° F. Ants stay in their nests when the temperature drops below 54° F. Still another temperature indicator is the cicada, which will not sing when the temperature is below 83° F.

If it is very hot and you can hear no insects at all, you can be fairly sure it is at least 106° F. All insects are silent above this temperature. If other signs tell you that there is also very high humidity, then you can expect some relief from the heat by late afternoon in the form of convection thundershowers.

Morning thunder is another hint of afternoon thundershowers. Campers and hikers would be wise to avoid low ground if they hear the sound of thunder early in the morning. When the atmosphere is hot and humid enough to cause an electrical discharge early in the day, the air will expand and rise, resulting in convection thundershowers. These showers never last long and cover a relatively small area. They bring relief by cooling the temperature of the ground and air, but they can cause local flash flooding. Pilots of light planes would be wise to avoid such areas lest they be buffeted by severe updrafts.

> Thunder in the morning
> Is a storm warning.

A mirage is another forewarning of a thunderstorm. Mirages are tricks that nature plays on your eyes when the air is very hot. Some people think mirages are seen only in the desert, but they can be seen anywhere, even at sea. In fact, you probably have seen them yourself. Have you ever been traveling down the highway in an automobile on a very hot summer day and seen what looked like puddles of water on the road ahead? Of course, when you got to them, you found that there were no puddles at all. They were mirages. A narrow layer of air near the surface of the road was much hotter than the surrounding air. This layer of air acted as a mirror and reflected the sky, making it look like water on the road. Desert mirages are the same, only larger. The air next to the ground gets overheated and reflects the distant horizon. If mountains, houses, ships, or trees are outlined against the sky along the horizon, they, too, will be reflected.

Mirages in the sky are caused by a very warm layer of air resting on top of a cold layer. This is called a temperature inversion, and it happens when cold winds run under warm air, forcing it upward, or when warm winds blow over cold air in areas of low pressure. Severe storms usually develop. Sailors have known this for a long time, and when they see a mirage, they lower their mainsails and prepare to ride out a furious storm.

Whenever a mirage appears in the sky, there could also be some clear-air turbulence. If the mirage grows, bends out of shape, or gets smaller, you will know the air is turbulent. Clear-air turbulence cannot be forecast or picked up by radar, so pilots of small aircraft would be wise to heed this warning:

When mirages appear;
Do not fly near.

When people don't know weather signs they sometimes get into trouble. Alexander the Great passed through a hot, dry, desert region of Pakistan on the way home with his army after a successful battle in India. His battle-weary men set up camp in a dry gully, the lowest spot available, in order to get some relief from the heat. A sudden thunderstorm and cloudburst caused a flash flood that drowned thousands of soldiers and horses and destroyed much valuable equipment. Alexander's men were either not very weather-wise or were too weary to notice the signs, for, although thunderstorms can happen suddenly, they do not develop without warning.

Sometimes people get taken in by unseasonably warm spells. Have you ever gone out without a coat in the early spring because the temperature had been in the seventies for several days, only to come home in very cold weather several hours later? This happens when the wind shifts suddenly to a north wind, bringing cooler weather and maybe even snow. (Winds are always named for the direction they come *from*).

Almost everyone enjoys very warm weather when it comes in February or March. "Nice weather we're having, isn't it?" is a familiar greeting during such a period.

But if a weather-wise person hears it, he is sure to reply, "Just a weather breeder!" He knows that the warm, moist air will soon meet cold arctic air, often resulting in violent weather.

In some mountainous areas of the Southwest, if it suddenly turns warm in the winter after several days of very cold weather, teachers dismiss the students and send them home, because they know a heavy snow will fall soon.

Temperature is important in predicting weather changes. It is also important in knowing how to dress. But temperature is not all you need to know. The amount of humidity in the air is also important. A hot day with high humidity feels hotter than a hot day with dry air. A cold day with high humidity seems colder.

Any day seems colder when there is a wind. A temperature of 30° F. with a twenty-five-mile-per-hour wind will have the same feeling and effect as a real temperature of zero degrees. This is called the wind-chill factor.

A temperature of 50° F. in the wintertime is quite warm. A twenty-five-mile-per-hour wind will reduce the temperature to a chilly 30° F. Many people have suffered from frostbite because they did not take the wind-chill factor into account. The wind-chill table given below will help you decide how you should dress on a windy day.

WIND-CHILL-FACTOR TABLE

Wind speed	Thermometer reading (in degrees Fahrenheit)						
	50	40	30	20	10	0	-10
	Temperature reduced to						
5 mph	48	37	27	16	7	-6	-15
10 mph	40	28	16	22	-9	-22	-34
15 mph	36	22	9	-6	-18	-31	-45
20 mph	32	18	3	-9	-24	-40	-52
25 mph	30	16	0	-15	-29	-45	-58
30 mph	28	13	-2	-18	-33	-49	-63
35 mph	27	11	-4	-20	-35	-52	-67
40 mph	26	10	-5	-21	-36	-54	-69

Eight

Wind and Weather

A group of girls on a canoe trip down the Illinois River learned that failing to read weather signs correctly can spoil a weekend outing. A storm hit their camp during the night, blowing down two of their tents.

"I can't understand it," their leader said. "The sky was so clear last night. We felt we could just reach up and touch the stars."

"The south breeze was so warm and gentle," added one of the girls.

The stars' looking brighter and nearer should have alerted them to the fact that the humidity was high and the pressure was dropping. But an even more certain warning of the approaching storm was the nice warm south wind.

When the wind is in the south,
The rain is in its mouth.

Wind is one of nature's most reliable weather signs. People long ago learned that the speed and direction of the wind would give them clues to approaching storms.

Wind is moving air. You can't see it, but you can feel it and you can see objects moved by it. You can see clouds scudding across the sky, leaves trembling on a bough, or smoke drifting lightly on a gentle breeze. Another time you see smoke blowing out in a straight line from a chimney, dust billowing up, or fallen leaves being hurled across the yard by a strong wind.

Differences in air pressure cause the wind to blow. Air, like water, flows from a region of high pressure to a region of low pressure. Low-pressure areas are created when warm air expands and rises. High-pressure areas have cold air, which is heavy and hugs the ground. When warm air rises, cold air flows in to fill up the space, causing wind. The difference between a high- and low-pressure area is usually not very great. But the greater the difference between the two pressure areas is, the stronger the wind will be. A small difference causes only a mild, gentle breeze.

Light winds point to pressure low,
But gales around the same do blow.

In our hemisphere air moves inward, counter-clockwise, toward the center of a low-pressure area. Imagine the atmosphere as a giant ocean of air. Lows

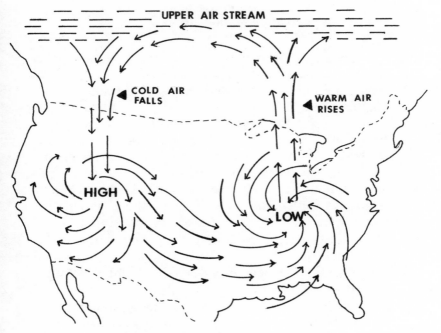

Air movement in the United States.

are like the eddies in water draining out of a bathtub. All of the air surrounding the low swirls around it the same way that water swirls in a bathtub.

High-pressure areas are like mountains of air. Winds blow in a clockwise direction and away from them toward the center of the low. Remember:

Counterclockwise round the low,
The whistling winds do back and blow.

Clockwise around the high,
The whistling winds will pass us by.

Long ago the captains of sailing ships paid close attention to winds. Without wind, their sailing ships would not move, as the Pilgrims were to find out. The captain of the *Mayflower* wasn't familiar with the winds of the world to the west. Both Columbus and Vespucci had sailed southward to pick up the trade winds, which pushed them to America; then they returned home by the prevailing westerlies, which blew toward Europe. The Pilgrims drifted into the wrong wind belt and had to wait days for a wind to blow them along. When one finally came, it was part of a severe storm that lasted eleven days and blew them to the wrong port.

After the American Revolution, all ships that sailed under the new American flag kept a detailed record of the types of weather they encountered. In their ships' logs they recorded the temperature of the air, the kinds of clouds, and the strength and direction of the winds on every voyage they made.

In 1842, a naval officer, Matthew Fontaine Maury, studied these logs and noticed that certain wind and weather patterns kept repeating themselves. He reasoned that if they had done so for the past sixty years, they would continue to do so, and so he began predicting weather for the navy. He also wrote a valuable manual for sailors about his findings. Many of the facts in the manual, such as the winds and the number of storms that might be expected in an area, are still used in determining steamship routes.

Maury's work confirmed what ancient sailors had

long known—that wind has a great deal to do with weather. Long before people knew about high- and low-pressure systems, sailors wrote rhymes about winds caused by them. This is a very old one:

A veering wind, fine weather.
A backing wind, foul weather.

A veering wind is one that shifts direction clockwise—for example, from southeast to south to southwest—and comes from a high pressure area. Winds from a high-pressure area usually bring fair weather.

A similar old saying is:

A backing wind says storms are nigh,
But a veering wind will clear the sky.

A backing wind is one that changes direction counterclockwise—for example, from southwest to southeast to east—and blows toward the center of a low.

Farmers put it this way:

When the wind changes against the sun,
Trust it not, for back 'twill run.

An easier way to remember it is:

Winds that swing against the sun,
And winds that bring the rain are one.
Winds that swing round with the sun,
Keep the rainstorm on the run.

Since the sun always moves from east to west, the wind that swings against the sun is shifting from west to east, and therefore around a low. Winds that change from east to west, as the sun does, blow from a high.

Meteorologists call low-pressure areas "storm centers" because they usually bring stormy weather. Low-pressure areas pull cold polar air masses down from northern Canada and the Arctic. Highs pull warm, moist tropical air up from the Gulf of Mexico and the Caribbean. Where these two air masses collide, heavy rain or snow falls. The meeting of warm, moist air and cold air masses always results in a storm.

The place where the two masses of air meet is called a front. If the cold air noses in under the warm air like a mole under the ground, it is called a cold front. The cold air forms a steep wedge from the ground to the sky, forcing the warmer air to rise, sometimes as much as five miles. Narrow bands of heavy thunderstorms or snowfalls usually occur. They may cover a strip five hundred miles long, but they seldom last longer than four hours. Thus the old saying:

> Rain before seven,
> Lift before eleven.

And another:

> You can tell between eleven and two
> What the weather will do.

If the morning is unsettled, wait until about eleven and you will know what the rest of the day will be like.

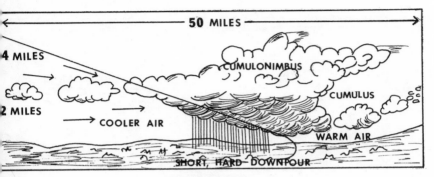

COLD FRONT

However, this is only true of a cold-front rain.

Sometimes the difference between the temperatures of the two air masses is not very much. Cold-front air can be 90° F. in the summer or -32° F. in the winter. It is cold only when compared to the air it is pushing upward. It would be more accurate to call it a "colder front." But remember: the greater the difference between the temperatures of the two air masses is, the more violent the storm will be.

It is called a warm front when a mass of warm air runs into a mass of cold air. Since warm air is lighter than cold air, it rides up over the cold air along a long, gradual slope. There will be a gentle rain or snow that may last all day and cover an area hundreds of miles wide, such as from Chicago to Buffalo.

Sometimes a mass of cold air undertakes another area of cold air. Warm, moist air is trapped above the two masses of cold air. This is called an occluded front. Occluded fronts cause a narrow band of violent storms

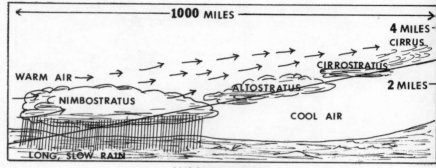

WARM FRONT

at the point where the two cold masses first meet and a wider area of cloudiness and rain or snow farther along the line.

Masses of air continuously move across North America from a more or less westerly direction to an easterly or northeasterly direction. High- and low-pressure systems move with the air masses. They usually move across the continent at about twenty to thirty miles per hour. The air you breathe out today will be 500 miles away tomorrow. St. Louis will have rain or snow one day. A few days later Philadelphia may have the same kind of weather. Benjamin Franklin discovered this movement of air in 1743 when he compared the weather in Philadelphia with the weather in Boston, where his brother lived.

By the end of World War I it was known that air masses move from west to east around the entire world in the Northern Hemisphere. During World War II, this knowledge made it possible for Allied weather stations to forecast a single day of calm weather for the invasion of Normandy. It also made it possible for the Nazi submarines in the ocean to the west of Europe to guarantee the German army a week of storms that would ground the Allied air forces during the Battle of the Bulge.

Meteorologists can usually predict where and when foul weather will arrive, because they know the exact location of the low and how far away it is. They sometimes seem to make errors in their forecasts because mountains, lakes, oceans, and even trees have some effect upon the movement of air so that air masses do not always move in a direct line or at a steady pace. Sometimes they do not move at all for several hours, and that is called a stationary front. If the land were perfectly flat, predicting weather would be easier.

Without studying a weather map you cannot know exactly where a low is located, but the wind can give you some clues. First, you need to know the direction from which the wind usually blows where you are. This is called the prevailing wind, and it produces the good weather for that area. In most places in the United States, the prevailing wind is from a westerly direction. It might shift toward the southwest in the summer or to the northwest in the winter, but in general it is from a westerly direction. This very old English weather verse will help you remember:

> When the smoke goes west,
> Good weather is past.
> When the smoke goes east,
> Good weather is neist [next].

Some winds, however, are local, sea breezes, for example. Areas bordering on a large lake or ocean, receive breezes from the water in the afternoon. Air over land heats more rapidly than air over water. It expands and rises. Then cool air from over the water moves in to fill up the space. After sunset the land cools faster than the water, and the air moves back over the water. Seamen say,

In by day,
Out by night.

There is a similar movement of cold air down into valleys at night and of warm air up onto the mountain slopes by day. Although such winds are normal for these areas, they have nothing to do with low-pressure systems. They can cause problems, however, for the unwary.

Members of a Scout troup, unaware of this natural flow of air, pitched their tents in a beautiful spot beside the Kanawha River at the foot of a mountain in West Virginia. During the night the wind flowing down the mountain and across the river dropped the temperature by 40 degrees, nearly freezing the unprepared Scouts. To avoid a similar mistake, remember this rule:

Valley temperature falls at night
To half the day's greatest height.

Local wind shifts do not give weather clues, but the way the wind shifts from the prevailing position can warn you, at least twenty-four hours in advance, when a low-pressure storm system is approaching. If the wind changes to counterclockwise, look for signs of pressure drop, which will indicate that a low-pressure system is near. Old sailors say:

> When the wind backs and the pressure falls,
> Be on your guard against gales and squalls.

You can determine the direction of the low from where you are, and thus the kind of weather to expect, by standing with your back to the wind and stretching out your arms sideways. Then make a 30-degree turn to the right. For example, if you are facing north, a 30-degree turn to the right would have you facing north-northeast. The center of the low-pressure system will be in the direction where your *left* hand is pointing. In this case it would be west-northwest. The low would pass north of you, and you would receive warm-front weather. The center of a high-pressure system will be in the direction to which your right hand points.

An old adage states, "Every wind has its weather." In general, this is true. Forget plans for a cookout or fishing trip the next day if the breeze is from the south, smoke is curling down to the ground, and the outline of distant hills is crisp and clear. Generally, if the pressure is falling, a wind from the south or southeast is a clue that a low is coming, and will pass north of you. When a low passes north of you, expect warm-front weather with warm southerly winds and long-lasting gentle rains within twenty-four hours or less. The wind will back, then veer after the center passes. Thus this old saying:

A southerly wind with showers of rain
Will bring the wind from the west again.

However, you can safely plan a weekend camping trip if the wind is from the south to southwest and the pressure is rising. You will have clearing and fair weather for several days.

But don't plan a boat trip for the next day if the wind is from the east or northeast. One summer a family was vacationing at the Lake of the Ozarks in Missouri. The weather had been perfect all week and the lake was almost mirror smooth. The Rodgers planned to spend their last day fishing off an island farther down the lake. They packed a picnic lunch and got an early start.

An old man stood on the deck silently watching as they loaded their gear.

"Going to be out long?" he asked.

"All day," Mr. Rodgers responded.

"Your craft is kind of small for rough waters, ain't it?" he asked.

"Yes, but it isn't rough today," Mr. Rodgers replied. There was only a light easterly breeze.

"Be a squall by midafternoon," warned the old man.

Rodgers laughed as he strapped on his life jacket. He had checked the Coast Guard advisory at the tackle shop, and there were no warning flags posted.

"We were so busy fishing we didn't notice the thunderheads building up in the northwest," Rodgers related later. "Then about noon the wind suddenly shifted to the northeast and the water became very choppy. We just made it back to our pier before the storm hit."

How did the old man know? The east wind told him. This was a typical cold-front squall. Winds from the east or northeast mean a low is passing south of you. Lows that pass to the south bring cold-front weather with heavy rains and possibly strong winds in the summer, or near-blizzard conditions in the winter, within twelve to twenty-four hours. New Englanders say:

> When the wind is in the east,
> It's good for neither man nor beast.
> If the wind comes out of the east,
> 'Twill rain in twenty-four hours at least.

Sportsmen say:

> Wind from the west, fishing is best;
> From the east fishing is least.

Cold fronts travel rapidly. After they pass, the air pressure will rise and the wind will back to the west, bringing fair weather.

> Winds blowing from the west
> Please everyone best.

But in summer, it is:

> When the wind is in the northwest,
> The weather is best.

Northwest winds bring cool, clear weather. They are usually dry and are accompanied by high pressure. If you want a raise in your allowance, you might try waiting for a northwest wind to ask for it, as this old saying suggests: "Do business with men when the wind is from the northwest." People are usually more agreeable and easier to deal with in fair weather, when they are feeling their best.

Texans say, "A day or two of strong south wind will blow in a 'norther.' "

North winds are the coldest, but they blow least often and seldom longer than one day at a time. They usually bring fair weather, unless a low has become stationary to the south.

During the American Revolution, General Washington used his wind knowledge to make battle plans. The roads had been muddy and impassable for several days. Then a sudden drop in temperature froze them solid, making it possible for Washington to move his artillery forward. Having read the signs correctly, Washington had expected that to happen and had made his plans accordingly. If he had not been prepared for the freeze when it came, the opportunity would have been lost.

You can predict a hard freeze anytime the wind is from the north or northwest from late fall to early spring, if the pressure is rising, the sky is clear, and a cold front has just passed to the south.

But remember, the way the wind shifts gives you a better clue than the direction from which it is blowing. The slightest shift is a hint of a weather change. The speed at which the wind blows is another clue.

Meteorologists use a wind vane or wind sock to determine the direction of the wind accurately and a special instrument called the anemometer to learn its

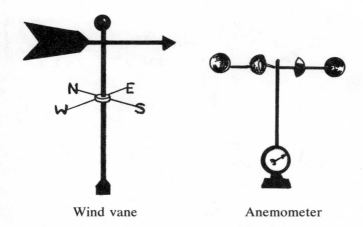

Wind vane   Anemometer

exact speed. You can determine the direction of the wind from smoke, flags, or even a piece of cloth tied to the top of a pole.

Cowboys watched the grass and leaves for a change in movement. When the wind veered, they took their cows to shelter.

If you see cows in a pasture all change position in the same direction, you will have a good indication of a wind shift and its direction. Cows don't like the wind to ruffle their hair, so they head into the wind.

Birds make pretty good weather vanes, too. Sea gulls are especially reliable on a beach, where there may be few other clues. Most birds sit facing the wind so their feathers will not get ruffled. They can take off more quickly into the wind.

You can learn many things about winds by observing birds. Modern scientists have discovered that birds

Cows head into the wind because they don't like it to ruffle their hair.

have an extraordinary knowledge of winds and weather. Some scientists believe that barometric pressure changes are the signals that tell birds it is time to migrate. Dropping pressure in the fall brings northerly winds, and rising pressure in the spring brings southerly winds, which make it easier for birds to fly in the proper direction. For example, small birds migrating south will wait until a cold front passes, and then, using the north or northwest wind as a tail wind, will fly out and let it carry them to their destination.

If you do not know north from south, you can use your watch as a compass. Sight down the hour hand toward the sun. The imaginary line from 12 through 6 will point to north, if you are on standard time. If you don't have a watch, you can put a stick in the ground and point the other end directly toward the sun until you can see no shadow. When the sun moves and a shadow appears, the direction in which the shadow points will be east. If it is dark or the sky is overcast, look for a tree

out in the open. The side that has moss growing on it
will be north.

Remember, winds are caused by pressure changes.
A combination of wind and pressure activity will give
you an accurate indication of what the weather will do.
The following chart shows you what to expect:

WIND DIRECTION	AIR PRESSURE	WEATHER
W	Low and rising	Clearing and colder
S to SW	Low and rising slowly	Clearing soon and fair for several days
Going to N	Low and rising rapidly	Clearing and colder
SW to NW	High and steady	Fair and little temperature change
SW to NW	High and rising rapidly	Fair followed by warmer weather, rain in 2 days
E to NE	High and falling slowly	Summer, fair; winter, rain in 24 hours
S to SE	High and falling rapidly	High wind with rain in 12 to 24 hours
SW to NW	High and falling slowly	Rain in 24 to 36 hours
E to NE	High and falling rapidly	Summer, rain and strong winds in 12 to 24 hours. Winter, snow and high winds.
SE to NE	High and falling rapidly	High winds, rain or snow

WIND DIRECTION	AIR PRESSURE	WEATHER
SE to NE	Low and falling slowly	Rain will continue for 1 or 2 days
SE to NE	Low and falling rapidly	Rain and high wind, clearing and cooler in 24 hours
S to SE	Low and falling rapidly	Severe storm soon
E to N	Low and falling rapidly	Northeast gales with heavy rain or snow
SE to E	High and falling	Rain in 1 day

Most winds die down after sunset because the surface air is not being heated. If winds do continue at night, they are usually strong and are a warning of stronger winds, and probably rain, the next day. Thus:

The winds of the day wrestle and fight
Longer and stronger than those of night.

and

Evening wind foretells tomorrow's weather.

There are many things that can give you clues to the speed of the wind. In 1805, before wind instruments had been invented, a man named Sir Francis Beaufort described the effect different wind speeds had on land and sea. His chart is still useful because most people think the wind is blowing harder than it actually is. The following table is based on this information.

Wind Speed (in miles per hour)	Effect
0–1	Water is mirror-smooth; smoke rises straight up.
2	Water has small wavelets but no crests; smoke drifts off to one side.
4–7	Light breeze can be felt on face; a flag waves gently but does not extend; leaves rustle; waves are short, pronounced.
8–12	Gentle breeze; leaves and twigs are in constant motion; flag extends out slightly from pole; sea crests begin to break with glassy foam.
13–18	Moderate breeze raises dust, dead leaves, loose paper, and small branches; sea waves become longer with many whitecaps; lake waters have pronounced ripples.
19–24	Small trees sway; flags extend straight out and beat; clothes on a line snap; crested wavelets appear on small lakes; lake wind warnings are issued; sea waves are larger, with white, foamy crests.
25–31	Large branches are in motion; difficulty walking against wind; buckets and boxes are blown around; sea waves are huge, with foam blowing in streaks; very choppy lake waters.
39–46	Twigs break off trees; large objects are hurled across the ground; sea waves roll and increase in height, with foam blowing in thick streaks.
over 45	Damage to trees and buildings; seek shelter.

Wind seldom blows at a steady pace. It is often accompanied by stronger gusts. A wind of twenty-five miles per hour can be accompanied by gusts of up to forty miles per hour. Watch out for these gusts if you plan a day on the water.

Generally, strong gusty winds are produced by fast-moving cold fronts with a great difference in air pressure. The storm area will cover a narrow strip and will soon pass. If the low-pressure system moves in slowly, it produces light steady winds. The rain and cloudiness will most likely last several hours.

> The sharper the blast,
> The sooner it's past.

No wind at all can also be a weather sign.

> No weather is ill,
> When winds are still.

But a calm is a warning of a change to come. It sometimes happens just before a wind shift along a cold-front squall line. This calm usually does not last long. Sometimes the rain starts before the strong winds do. In this case, be prepared for a gale. A calm occurs when the low pressure system passes directly over you. The whirling winds of the low-pressure system can trigger violent storms, as is noted in this old sailor's verse:

> If rain comes before the wind,
> Lower your topsails and take them in;

If the wind comes before the rain,
Lower your topsails and hoist them again.

Indian summer is a different kind of calm. It lasts
for a long period and covers a wide area. Such calms are
sometimes called "weather breeders," because no
calm will last.

Perhaps the first sign of a weather change after a
long calm will be winds moving clouds high up in the
sky. Meteorologists know that winds aloft soon become
surface winds. Sometimes you see clouds going in the
opposite direction to ground winds. This is an indication of a cold front moving in. You can expect rains to
follow soon, as this proverb points out:

If clouds fight the wind,
A storm will soon begin.

Nine

Sky Signs

Charles A. Lindbergh's knowledge of winds and clouds helped to make his solo flight across the Atlantic in 1927 a success. In his tiny plane, Lindbergh had no radio contact with the ground. There was no way for him to know weather conditions ahead except from the clues he saw in the sky. He nearly lost his life early in the flight when ice covered the wings of his plane as he flew into a thunderhead. He turned back quickly and learned to avoid all other threatening clouds by flying around them. In so doing, he made the first successful flight across the Atlantic.

No pilot of small aircraft should consider flying without some knowledge of winds and clouds. Weather-advisory reports are made periodically throughout the day, but as you have learned, storm cells can develop very rapidly in any given area. Clouds can warn you when this is happening.

People throughout the ages have scanned the heavens for weather clues. Many warnings of weather changes can be found there. Of all nature, the sky is the easiest to read and tells the most. Clouds announce all of our bad weather and most of our good. They are among nature's most reliable weather signs and are always there when you need them.

Everything about a cloud is important. You can learn something from its shape, color, and size; from its rate of growth and change; from its height; and from the speed and direction of its movement. Meteorologists consider them important elements in weather forecasting.

Clouds can give you an early warning of wind shifts. When you see high clouds sailing across the sky in a different direction from lower clouds, you can be sure the wind will change in the direction of the high clouds within a few hours.

Just as every weather has its wind, every weather has its cloud.

> If clouds be bright,
> 'Twill clear tonight;
> If clouds be dark,
> 'Twill rain, do hark?

There are many kinds of clouds. Meteorologists have given them names such as cirrus, which means very high, and nimbus, which means rain.

Cumulus clouds are soft, white clouds that look

Cumulus clouds
Courtesy Union Pacific Railroad

like globs of whipped cream or marshmallow. When they are small and drift across a bright-blue sky in an easterly or southeasterly direction, they are usually a sign of fair weather, especially if they are high.

"The higher the cloud, the dryer the air," the ancients said. That is because dry air must ascend much higher than humid air before reaching the dew point. These high clouds are the ones that sometimes form pictures. They usually appear just after a low-pressure system has passed through, and are called cirrocumulus.

High-flying clouds don't threaten immediate rain, but low clouds almost always do. When low cumulus clouds begin to grow before noon and then pile up into towering columns with dark, flat bases during the early afternoon, you can expect thunderstorms, lightning, and possibly hail with strong gusts of wind by late afternoon, but with clearing before sundown. These are typical convection clouds. The Zuni Indians say:

> When clouds rise in terraces of white,
> Soon will the country of the corn priests
> Be pierced with the arrows of rain.

On hot, humid days the sun beats down on open fields or desert floors, and the ground gets very hot. The ground in turn heats the moist air, which expands and rises. When the air has risen high enough to cause the moisture to condense, a cloud begins to form. If the ground is very hot, the column of moist air keeps on

Cumulus clouds building up into thunderheads.

Courtesy National Oceanic and
Atmospheric Administration

rising, building into a towering cumulus cloud. Sometimes the cloud towers up thousands of feet into the
sky. As the cloud stacks up, water vapor condenses
into raindrops and begins to fall. If the cloud goes high
enough, hail or snow may form, but most of the time it
will melt before it reaches the ground because of the hot
air below the cloud. Remember:

> A round-top cloud with flattened base,
> Carries rainfall in its face.

Or, as another folk verse says:

> When clouds appear like hills and towers
> The earth's refreshed by frequent showers.

Altocumulus, which are medium high-clouds that
make the sky look as though a tractor had plowed
through a field of snow, are a forewarning of a weather
change, as are cirrocumulus clouds, the very high, tiny,
white, fluffy clouds that ripple across the whole sky like
sand on a beach. You can expect high winds from the
northwest and possibly rain or snow within fifteen to
twenty hours. These clouds are a sign that a cold front is
on the way. As the cold front moves in, the shifting
winds coming with it break up existing clouds and give
the sky the dappled look that sailors called "mackerel
sky" and farmers called "buttermilk sky." Thus we
have:

> Mackerel sky, mackerel sky,
> Never long wet, never long dry.

Altocumulus clouds

Courtesy National Oceanic and Atmospheric Administration

Cirrocumulus clouds

Mackerel clouds in the sky,
Expect more wet than dry.

Medium-high cumulus clouds that rapidly begin to mass together with little warning are a definite clue that a cold front is approaching. Look for heavy thundershowers or snowstorms and possibly high winds within twelve hours. Sometimes these patches of clouds move in at night. The cloud patches blot out some of the stars, making it look as if the rest are huddled together. So we have this verse:

Stratocumulus and altocumulus clouds
Courtesy NOAA

When stars begin to huddle,
The earth will soon become a puddle.

Very low, cauliflower-shaped clouds with dark ragged bases and high, flat, anvil-shaped tops are cumulonimbus clouds. They are also called thunderheads. When you see a line of them piling up across the sky from north-northwest to west, be prepared for a wind shift soon to the south or southwest and heavy rain squalls accompanied by lightning and thunder, or,

Cumulonimbus clouds

Courtesy NOAA

in winter, very heavy snowfalls. These cloud mountains may build up five miles high. Some are taller than any mountain on earth.

When mountains and cliffs in clouds appear,
Some sudden and violent showers are near.

The taller the cloud, the more violent the storm. Thunderstorms are caused by powerful electrical charges building up inside the clouds. They are discharged in a tremendous spark, something like the sparks that occur when you pull two blankets apart in the dark, only a thousand times bigger. You see the spark as a flash of lightning. A few seconds later you hear the roll of thunder. If you have heard the thunder, you can relax. You know the lightning did not strike you.

Sometimes you might want to know how far away the storm is. There is a way you can tell approximately how far away the lightning is. If you have seen a woodcutter on a hillside or a carpenter some distance away, you may have noticed that you could see the ax or hammer hit a few seconds before you heard it. That is because sound travels slower than light. By counting the number of seconds between a flash of lightning and the thunder, you can figure out how far away the storm is. If you do not have a watch, count "lightning one, lightning two, lightning three," and so on. It takes about one second to say "lightning one." The speed of sound is about 1 mile every five seconds. To determine the approximate distance of the lightning, figure 1 mile for every 5 seconds counted. If you counted 12 sec-

When the huge amount of atmospheric electricity that builds up in storm clouds is discharged, the result is a flash of lightning.

Courtesy Leighton Venn

onds, the storm would be almost two and a half miles away. Sometimes thunder can be heard twenty miles away, but it usually only carries about ten miles.

If you see the lightning to the northwest, west, or southwest, the storm will be moving toward you at approximately 30 miles per hour. In that case, you will have about five minutes to find shelter. If the lightning is in the north, east, or south, it will probably miss you and you need not seek shelter. However, keep your eyes and ears open. Another storm could form, and it might not miss you.

The color of lightning can give you a clue to the type of storm approaching and whether it is a threat to you. Red and green lightning mean an intense and severe thunderstorm. Yellow lightning is far away, probably too far to hear the thunder, and it will most likely pass north or south of you. This folk rhyme gives you the rule:

> Yaller gal, yaller gal,
> Flashing through the night,
> Summer storms will pass you,
> Unless the lightning's white.

The location of the lightning is another clue.

Lightning in the west or northwest will reach you.
Lightning in the south or southeast will pass you by.

If the air is very muggy and oppressive (hot and humid), watch the clouds carefully. Cumulonimbus clouds sometimes become a dirty greenish-black or have a yellowish tinge when the air is very hot and humid. They roll and churn like a huge kettle of boiling water and bulge downward like an upside-down cumulus. When you see this kind of cloud, seek shelter immediately, especially if the wind has shifted suddenly. These clouds, which are called cumulomannatus, signal the approach of a hailstorm or tornado, and much lightning. Often, when seen from below, they look like clusters of giant grapes. Watch for increased wind noise, heavy rain, hail, and lots of thunder and lightning, as well as a funnel.

Tornadoes occur only with cold fronts. They are caused when much colder air collides with warm, moist

The funnel of a tornado can do tremendous damage, and you must take shelter if one is heading in your direction.

Courtesy NOAA

Cumulomannatus clouds

Courtesy NOAA

air. They develop rapidly and move very fast, seldom staying in any one place more than a minute, but they do a tremendous amount of damage. Fortunately, the path of a tornado is not usually more than a few blocks wide and only a few miles long. If you see a funnel on the ground heading your way, the best thing to do is go to a cellar or overhanging cliff, if one is near, and if not, lie down in the lowest depression you can find until it has passed.

At night you will have to rely on your ears alone. You can usually hear the roar of a funnel about two miles away. That would give you about three minutes to take cover. When in doubt, don't wait. Occasionally funnels form directly overhead and give no advance warning sound.

Each weather front has its own special kind of clouds. Cumulus clouds, which go with cold fronts, almost never produce long rainfalls. Only stratus clouds, the flat, gray, layered, sheetlike clouds, bring long rains. Stratus clouds go with warm fronts. Occluded fronts have a combination of both.

The first clue of a warm front coming will be many beautiful white streamers that look like giant ostrich plumes or huge jet contrails sailing very high across a clear blue sky. They are a form of cirrus cloud, and are so high they are made of ice crystals even on the hottest summer day. A steady stream of curling wisps racing eastward across the sky at a very rapid pace (100 to 200 miles per hour) is a forewarning that a storm with brisk winds is coming within twenty to thirty hours. Meteorologists tell us that these cirrus clouds, which sailors call "mares' tails" or "hen scratches," have been blown in by high wind currents from a warm-front

"Mares' tails," a form of cirrus cloud
Courtesy NOAA

storm system. High winds aloft mean weather changes close to the earth in two or three days. Sailors have used these clouds as weather clues for centuries. Even ancient Greek sailors knew that:

Mares' tails, mares' tails
Make tall ships carry low sails.

And English sailors chanted:

Hen's scratches and filly tails,
Get ready to reef your top sails.

Stratus clouds

Courtesy NOAA

Don't count on a weekend out-of-doors if the sky is full of cobwebby sheets of cirrus clouds on Friday. This is a sign that a large warm-front storm system is getting closer. Be prepared for rain within twenty-four hours.

> Cobwebs in the sky
> Means rain nearby.

Or, as they say in the Midwest when the sky is full of wispy, veil-like cirrus clouds:

> Trace in the sky the painter's brush,

The winds around you soon will rush.

A ring around the sun or moon is still another sign of a warm-front storm moving in. A large ring is a warning that rain or snow will likely arrive in less than twenty-four hours. Large whitish rings, called halos, occur when the sun or moon shines through cirrostratus clouds. These clouds are thin sheets of ice crystals. They may or may not cover the entire sky. They are so high up you can barely see them until they pass under the moon or sun and make the halo. These clouds are formed when the nose of the warm front is forced to rise to icy heights, five miles or more above the ground. People have long recognized halos as a warning of bad weather.

The Indians said, "When the sun is in his house, it will rain soon."

Farmers used to say:

> If the moon shows a silver shield,
> Don't be afraid to reap your field;
> But if she rises haloed round,
> Soon you'll walk on flooded ground.

Sailors said: "Last night the moon had a golden ring. Tonight there is no moon."

Shepherds believed: "The moon with a circle brings water in her beak." And: "The circle of the sun wets the shepherd."

Still other people say:

> When the moon wears a halo

Halo shining through cirrostratus clouds.
Courtesy NOAA

Around her head, she will cry
Before morning and her tears
Will reach you before tomorrow.

Actually, this verse is more true of a corona than a halo. Coronas are smaller, rainbow-colored rings that can be seen when the sun shines through altostratus clouds. Altostratus clouds are made of water droplets and are lower than cirrostratus clouds. A corona, which is formed farther along a warm front, is a warning that a storm is near, as this very old weather verse says:

When the wheel is far,
The storm is n'ar.
When the wheel is n'ar,
The storm is far.

Translated, this means:

When the circle is small,
The storm is near.
When the circle is big,
The storm is far.

Midwesterners say it more simply: "The smaller the ring, the nearer the wet."

When the corona disappears and the moon or sun shines through the clouds like a light bulb shining through a frosted glass pane, it means the altostratus clouds have dropped lower and become thicker. People used to say:

When sun and moon become a blur,
Within six hours rains will stir.

When altostratus clouds change to flat, dark-gray nimbostratus clouds that cover the whole sky, pack your gear and head for home. If the wind is from the northeast, east, southeast, or south, you can expect the

Altostratus clouds

Courtesy NOAA

long-lasting heavy rain of a warm front. But if the wind comes from another direction, you may receive only a light drizzle.

A warm-front storm approaches slowly, sending out warnings long in advance. It also passes slowly. Thunderstorms of a cold front form more quickly with less warning and pass quickly.

Nimbostratus clouds

Courtesy NOAA

Rain long foretold, long last;
Short notice, soon past.

Some historians tend to blame Napoleon's defeat
at Waterloo on an unexpected rainfall the night before
his planned surprise attack, which made the fields and
roads so wet and muddy that his artillery and cavalry
could not move swiftly enough. Actually, no rain comes

without some advance warning. A night rain hard enough to make the ground that muddy certainly gave at least twenty-four hours' advance warning. If the army was surprised, it was because they were not watching the sky for signs well-known long before Napoleon's time.

Other things in the sky besides clouds can indicate weather changes. Sunrises and sunsets have been used as weather indicators throughout the ages. A red sky is quite noticeable even to people who spend most of their days indoors. It is probably the weather sign known by more people today than any other. There are two kinds of red sky: one that is a deep angry red, caused by large amounts of water vapor in the air, and a gentle rose-red sky in which there is a lack of moisture, but which contains many dust particles.

When you see a rose-red or pinkish sunset, you can be fairly sure that there will be fair weather for the next several hours. It is an indication that there is stable air for many miles to the west, which is the direction from which our storms usually come. A yellow or greenish sunset indicates extremely dry, clear air, and the probability of clear weather is even greater. Thus:

> Glimpse you e'er the green ray,
> Count the morrow a fine day.

On the other hand, a violently red sunrise is a warning of an approaching storm. Very humid air has been pulled up from the Gulf of Mexico by an approaching low-pressure system. This proverb has been used by sailors for thousands of years:

Red sky at night is a sailor's delight.
Red sky in the morning, sailors take warning!

This saying is so reliable it has been included in naval officers' textbooks. Jesus had it in mind when He spoke to the Pharisees and Sadducees. You may be more familiar with this verse:

Evening red and weather fine,
Morning red, of rain's a sign.

This truth is so well known around the world it is difficult to believe that there is anyone who has not heard it. Yet people still get caught because they don't heed it. A California couple, who often take leisurely drives into the mountains, got up early one March Sunday so they could enjoy the sunrise at the top of a mountain.

The glowing ball of orange-red poking up over the mountains and painting the sky fiery red was even more spectacular than they had anticipated.

They continued their drive along the winding roads until they came to a small inn high up the slopes, and stopped there for a leisurely lunch. When they came out again, they noticed that the clouds had closed in. It soon began to snow. By midafternoon they had to stop and wait for a snowplow to get them out.

A brilliantly red sunrise will produce a storm before the day is over, winter or summer. Shepherds used to say:

An evening gray and a morning red
Will send the shepherd wet to bed.

Evening gray and morning red
Make the shepherd hang his head.

A gray sunset means rain, because it is caused by a stratus cloud sheet, a sign that a low-pressure system is moving in. A gray sunrise, however, means clear weather if it follows a rosy sunset. The grayness is usually caused by a gray mistiness, the result of radiation cooling off the earth during the night. This can only happen in fine, clear weather. Thus we have these sayings:

Evening red and morning gray
Sets the traveler on his way;
Evening gray and morning red
Brings down rain upon his head.

The evening red and the morning gray
Is the sign of a bright and cheery day;
The evening gray and the morning red,
Put on your hat, or you'll wet your head.

And this one for a fair day:

Evening red and morning gray
Two sure signs of one fine day.

This ancient-Greek one is a bit different:

Red sun at night,
Next day will be fair.
Sun pale or white,
Sailors beware.

A pale sun or moon is a sign of a cold front moving in, and there is a probability of rain. The pale appearance can be caused either by dust particles picked up by strong winds or by cirrus clouds blown from the tops of distant thunderheads. Either is a forewarning of a storm. Therefore:

> If the sun goes pale to bed,
> 'Twill rain tomorrow, it is said.

When the moon and stars are covered by a thin film of cirrus clouds, they look faint, seem far away, and twinkle with a bluish cast. Much dust in the air makes the moon look like a huge red ball. A very old Roman proverb states:

> Pale moon rains; red moon blows;
> White moon neither rains nor blows.

The Zuni Indians say, "A red moon has water in his eye," and:

> The moon, her face if red be
> Of water speaks she.

But don't judge the color of the moon until it is well up into the sky, because a full moon is often orange or red-orange when it first appears over the horizon.

A white moon and bright stars are signs of fair weather. Old farmers say:

> Clear moon,
> Frost soon,

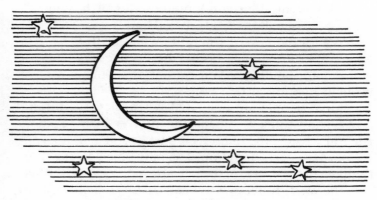

A clear, sharp-looking moon and stars are a sign of winds high up in the atmosphere.

because it frosts only on clear nights. But when the moon and stars are exceptionally brilliant and clear you can expect windy weather. Normal amounts of dust particles in the earth's atmosphere give the moon a fuzzy outline and cause stars to "twinkle." High-speed winds aloft clear the air and make the points of a new moon appear sharp and distinct. Since upper-level winds soon become surface winds, we have the proverb: "Sharp horns on the moon do threaten windy weather."

A Missouri farmer was a firm believer in this old proverb, but sometimes nature's warnings don't come soon enough to give you time to do all you need to do.

"We'd better get that wheat cut this morning," the farmer told his son. "There were sharp horns on the moon last night. A big wind could shatter all the grain.''

They got half the field cut and barely made it to the stable with the horses when the wind hit. In less than ten minutes it flattened his hay barn and every blade of wheat left standing. Even a rainbow could not have brought him joy at that point.

Most people are delighted when they see a rainbow. They think it means the rain is over. That is generally true if the rainbow is east of you and the wind is from a westerly direction. The only time you can see a rainbow in the east is in the late afternoon, when the sun is in the west. Rainbows are caused by sunlight shining through water droplets in the air. Since in North America most rains travel from west to east, a rainbow to the east of you means that the rain clouds have already passed by.

If the rainbow is in the west don't start out on a fishing trip, unless you like to fish in the rain. Rainbows can only be seen in the west in the early morning, when the sun is in the east. That means the rain clouds are in the west, or to your windward slide. Rain will probably reach you soon.

> A rainbow in the morning
> Is shepherds' warning;
> A rainbow at night
> Is shepherds' delight.

Sailors said it this way:

> Rainbow to windward,
> Foul falls the day;

> Rainbow to leeward,
> Rain runs away.

American Indians say:

> Rainbows in west bring light showers,
> Rainbows to east promise good hunting.

Go ahead with outdoor plans for the next day if you can see the sun as it sets, even though the rest of the sky is overcast. When the sun sets clear, more often than not the next day will be fair. A clear sky is a dry sky. You can usually expect fair weather for at least the next twenty-four hours if the sun breaks through the clouds or blue sky begins to show. Midwesterners say, ''If you can see enough blue to make an old woman's apron, the weather will clear.''

That is true, however, only if the clouds are breaking up and showing patches of blue in the west. Clouds getting higher, whiter, and becoming fewer in number by late afternoon are another sign of good weather ahead.

By combining the messages of the sky with wind direction and animal signs, you should be able to forecast the weather for the next day well enough to keep from being caught in a blizzard or severe thunderstorm. At least you can do as well as the old fellows standing on a street corner on a cloudy, threatening day.

''You think it will rain?'' one asks, wiping the sweat from his brow.

The other squints his eyes, looks at the large cumulus clouds building up to the west, and drawls, ''If it don't, it will miss an awfully good chance."

Or, if that fails, you can fall back on this old weather saying:

In wet weather it rains without half trying;
All signs fail in dry weather.

Ten

Myths and Observations

Many old sayings were used to predict weather for the next season. Most of them do not have a scientific explanation. Some of them are based upon long observation and seem to be generally true. Others are pure myth.

One example almost everyone is familiar with is: "If the groundhog sees his shadow on February 2, we will have six more weeks of bad weather." This piece of folklore came to us from the early German settlers.

Early Christians believed that the weather on a saint's day was an indication of the weather for the season. One of these days was Candlemas Day, the Feast Day of Saint Mary, which falls on February 2. They believed that if it rained on Candlemas Day there would be an early spring. Germans believed that if the woodchuck, or groundhog, saw the sun and came out of his burrow on Candlemas Day, he would see his shadow, be frightened by it, and return to his burrow. Winter would then continue for another six weeks. If he didn't see his shadow, he would stay out and spring would be early.

Protestant Germans who settled in Pennsylvania dropped the religious significance of the day, but kept the observance of Groundhog's Day on February 2. People in Pennsylvania Dutch country and other parts of the United States where large numbers of Germans settled continue to celebrate this day by keeping groundhogs. They watch to see what they do on their day. If a groundhog wakes up, walks out of its cage, and does not return, they say there will be an early spring. If

A groundhog and its shadow.

he sees his shadow or returns to the cage, they expect six more weeks of winter.

Now everyone knows that neither the groundhog nor the second day of February has a thing to do with the weather. The only basis of truth in this saying is that generally, if January and early February are mild, you can expect some wintry weather in March. Conversely, if there has been bad weather from January through late February, spring will often be early. That is the basis for the old saying, "If March comes in like a lion, it will go out like a lamb."

Perhaps the best use of these bits of folklore is to remind people that fruit trees and flowers that blossom early due to a mild February will most likely get frostbitten in late March or early April. A continuous covering of snow in northern states during January and February will delay the blossoming of the fruit trees until after the killing frosts have ended. It also prevents the frequent freezing and thawing of the ground, which damages winter grains, and guarantees plenty of ground moisture at the right time. One popular saying is: "A year of snow, a year of plenty." And old farmers say:

> If you see grass in January,
> Lock your grain in your granary.
>
> A February spring is worth nothing.
> A late spring never deceives.

Generally, you can be fairly sure spring has arrived when the groundhogs wake up and come out of their winter sleeping places, migrating birds return, frogs and toads dig up through the mud, snakes and turtles come out of their winter nests, butterflies or moths can be seen flitting about, and many spring flowers are in bloom. If you notice these signs earlier than usual, you can safely predict that there will be no more severe winter weather. Of course, in northern states there may be one or two killing frosts in April, even with an early spring.

The Apaches said, "Early insects, early spring, good crops."

For centuries people have tried to predict the next season's weather on the basis of particular holidays. Of course there is no truth to the saying that if it rains on Easter Sunday it will rain seven Sundays in a row, though it may seem that it does, especially if it is a wet spring. However, an unusually wet spring is often followed by a hot, dry summer. So there is some truth to the saying that "He who sows his crops in rain will reap in tears."

Similarly, there is no basis for the saying that if the weather is bad on Palm Sunday it will bring bad crops.

There are many weather myths about Christmas, for example:

A warm Christmas, a cold Easter.
A cold Christmas, a warm Easter.

Many people confidently believe that the twelve days of Christmas foretell what the weather will be for the next twelve months. Others hold it is the first twelve days of January that tell the weather for the year.

These weather myths are fun to know, but don't stake your future on them.

Signs from nature are often used to predict a mild or severe winter. One of the best known of these signs concerns the hairy black caterpillar known as the woolly bear, which is the larva stage of the tiger moth. It has a wide brown band around its middle. Caterpillar watchers say that when the woolly bear grows a heavy coat, it means the winter will be hard. On the other hand, they say, a wide brown band means a mild winter. The wider the band, the milder the winter. If the caterpillars have no brown band at all, the winter will be severe. There is no scientific fact on which to base this belief, but a scientist investigated it for several years, and it seems to be fairly accurate.

Many people say that when the woolly bear caterpillar grows a heavy coat, the winter will be long and hard.

There are many more sayings that have no basis in scientific fact that we know of. Try observing them for yourself for a number of years to test their accuracy. If they prove accurate seventy-five percent of the time, they can be considered reasonably good indicators for long-range forecasts.

Weather prophets in the Southeast say, "Fog in August indicates a severe winter and plenty of snow." The number and density of the fogs are supposed to indicate the number of times it will snow and the depth of the snow. There may be a grain of truth to this belief, since fogs in August could indicate cold arctic air coming farther south earlier than usual, which could cause a colder fall. Anyway, Sarah Crane believes it. After a foggy August, her grandmother told her the winter of 1976 would be a real wingdinger, and sure enough, it was the worst winter up to that time in the mountains of Tennessee.

American Indians put great stock in animal signs, which they taught to white settlers. The height and strength of muskrat or beaver houses, rabbit lairs, and hornet nests indicated the severity of the winter, they claimed. Northwest Indians say the winter will be severe if ruffed grouse grow heavier-than-usual fringes on their toes. "Grouse grow snowshoes to walk in heavy snow," they say.

In the northern states it is said that if field mice move into barns or houses early in the fall and wild animals have thicker fur than usual, there will be a long, cold winter.

In the Southwest, restless and aggressive snakes mean a hard winter. And in the South, spiders and other insects moving indoors ahead of schedule are an indication of an early winter.

Many old weather prophets declare leaves and plants are the most reliable weather indicators. In the South they say thick and tight corn shucks and unusually thick nutshells mean a cold, rough winter.

Midwesterners say that if the bark peels on sycamore and birch trees in the late fall you will have a mild winter. If it stays on and gets thicker, the winter will be severe. If trees split their bark during the winter, there will be a hot, dry spring. Others say:

> When leaves drop early,
> Fall will be short and mild.
> When leaves fall late,
> Winter will be severe.

> If on the trees the leaves still hold,
> The coming winter will be cold.

This only applies, they explain, to trees that normally drop their leaves early in autumn.

Midwestern farmers swear that unusually heavy and early peach or berry crops are a warning of an early and severe winter. They also claim root crops grow deeper before a hard winter. Maybe that can be explained by this centuries-old proverb:

> Whenever there is much snow,
> A fruitful crop generally grows.

In New England, people set great store on the

amount of moss covering the north side of oak trees. If it is thick, they say there will be heavy snows. But if the moss dries up in the fall, the winter will be mild.

This is a very old English saying that many people still believe in:

> Onion's skin very thin,
> Mild winter coming in;
> Onion's skin thick and tough,
> Coming winter cold and rough.

Actually the thickness of the skin on an onion depends upon the amount of rain during the growing season rather than upon the coming winter. However, the amount of rain in the growing season may have some bearing upon the kind of weather that will be experienced during the following winter.

Here's another old proverb:

> As high as the weeds grow
> So will the bank of snow.

Some claim, "If there's thunder and lightning in January, there will be frost in April," or "Thunder in February means frost in May." Farmers plant their crops accordingly. They also claim, "The first frost in the fall always comes six months after the first thunder of spring."

Midwestern farmers say, "If it rains on Monday, it will rain three other days that same week," and "If it rains while the sun is shining, it will rain the next day, too." Of course, to find out if these sayings are true,

Some people believe that when chickens take cover, there will be a short, hard downpour.

one would need to keep an accurate record for many years.

Some people claim they can tell how long it will rain by the way their chickens act. If they stay out in the rain, it will last all day, but if they take cover, it will be a short, hard downpour.

Early settlers put great stock in the moon. They believed if the crescent moon tipped down, the weather would be wet. If it cupped up, the weather would be dry.

Tipped moon—wet;
Cupped moon—dry.

According to the *Old Farmer's Almanac*, if the new moon comes on Sunday, there will be a flood before the month is over. If it changes on Monday, the weather will be fair. If it changes on Saturday, the next twenty days will be wet and windy. The nearer the moon's change is to midnight, the fairer the weather for the next seven days, and the nearer to noon, the more wet and foul the next seven days.

The belief that the phases of the moon are related to weather has been one of the most long-lived beliefs of folklore. Theophrastus wrote, "The beginnings and ends of the lunar month are apt to be stormy." Many farmers will not plant their crops unless the moon is at the right stage. "Otherwise," say those that follow this practice, "rains and growing temperatures will not follow." Root crops are planted in the dark side of the moon. Leaf and grain crops are planted in the light side of the moon (new moon). If the procedure is reversed, they claim, root crops all go to leaves and leaf crops go to roots. They also pay attention to the proper zodiac signs. For these, one must consult an almanac, such as the *Old Farmer's Almanac* of 1961, from which this quote is taken:

> Go plant the beans when the moon is light
> And you will find that is right.
>
> Plant the potatoes when the moon is dark
> And to this you'll always hark."

Probably the first people who looked to the moon when they planted were the early Babylonians. Their crops had to be in the ground before the rivers flooded, or not at all. Since they lived in an area with little seasonal change and had no calendar, they watched the skies to devise a way to tell when the rains could be

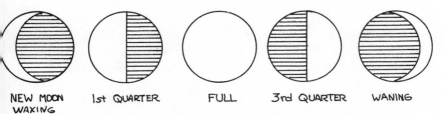

NEW MOON WAXING   1st QUARTER   FULL   3rd QUARTER   WANING

MOON PHASES

expected. They discovered that the moon and other heavenly bodies had regular movements. They recorded all this information on clay tablets, thereby making the first almanac.

Almanacs of one kind or another were used around the world throughout history. The Egyptians wrote one on a block of wood, and even the American Indians had zodiac tables. Sailors used almanacs for navigation, as did Columbus on his voyage to the New World. In early colonial days people valued their almanacs second only to their Bibles.

The first almanac in America was printed in 1639. These early almanacs recorded the movements of heavenly bodies and gave moon phases, planting guides, and forecasts of weather. They also contained weather proverbs and household hints. Benjamin Franklin's *Poor Richard's Almanack* is one of the best known of the colonial almanacs. The oldest still in existence today is the *Old Farmers' Almanac*, first printed in 1793. It has been printed continuously ever since.

Many people scoff at the idea that the moon has

anything to do with weather and planting. "You plant in the moon," they say. "I'll plant in the ground."

However, meteorologists studied weather records of more than fifteen hundred weather stations for a fifty-year period to find out if there was a relationship between very heavy rainfalls and moon phases. They concluded that heavy rains or snowfalls come most often during the first and third weeks after a full moon.

The Jewish people have claimed for three thousand years that it never rains on Yom Kippur, the Hebrew Day of Atonement, which always falls in the second week of the lunar month.

All weather sayings should be checked for accuracy. They should not be confused with weather signs, which have been proved reliable. Some of the sayings are obviously not true. It *might* rain "when a cat sits in a window and washes its face," but not always, because cats sit in windows and wash their faces almost every day.

Another old saying that definitely is not true is that "lightning never strikes twice in the same place." Actually it often does. A barn in Missouri was struck by lightning and burned to the ground. The farmer felt safe in rebuilding the barn on the same foundation. He believed it would never be struck again. Two years later lightning struck the new barn and it also burned down. And there is a church in England that has been struck by lightning six times.

Weather signs are a heritage from our ancestors. Farmers, shepherds, woodsmen, sailors, Indians, and other people who worked out-of-doors kept track of weather changes and of plant and animal behavior.

Their weather knowledge was an accumulation of hundreds of years of observation. Not all of their signs fit every section of the country, but with study and observation you will soon find which ones fit your area. You should not expect to know in a few days what it took your ancestors centuries to learn, but with practice you will be able to predict your local weather for the next few hours. Weather observation is a good hobby. You can make a lifelong habit of observing nature.

You can also discover signs of your own. Listen to daily weather reports. Each time rain has been forecast for the next twenty-four-hour period, go outside and observe nature. See what the plants and animals are doing. Observe the sky. How many clouds are there and what do they look like? What is their shape and height? In what direction are they moving? What changes are taking place? What is the direction and effect of the wind?

Keep a weather diary. Write down all of the conditions you have just observed. Report what the weatherman said about barometric pressure. Record the weather that actually occurred.

Whenever you think you have discovered a new weather sign, be sure to test it for validity. It must happen at least eight times out of ten. You should also test any new weather signs you hear from others. Is there a scientific explanation for a plant's or animal's behavior? Could it have been caused by high humidity? Might it be from a pressure drop?

Try to predict the local weather for the next twenty-four hours from the information you have learned. Don't try to make a prediction on one piece of evidence. Look around you. If it is a valid sign, you will surely find several others indicating the same thing.

Never regard any piece of information as a separate or isolated event. Remember, each piece of information is a part of a whole. These pieces can be fitted and used together like pieces of a jigsaw puzzle to produce a forecast. Check your predictions against those made by meteorologists as reported locally on radio and television, or in the newspaper. You will soon be able to predict your local weather with surprising accuracy. Practice will improve your skill and sharpen your weather sense.

Fortunately you do not need to worry about day-by-day accuracy, as our ancestors did. But a certain amount of accuracy can be very useful if you love the out-of-doors and are a camping, hiking, fishing, boating, or biking enthusiast. You can also amaze your friends and family with your knowledge.

Index